A GUIDE TO

JULIUS CAESAR

The Shakespeare Handbooks

Guides available now:

- Antony & Cleopatra
- As You Like It
- Hamlet
- Henry IV, Part 1
- Julius Caesar
- King Lear
- Macbeth
- A Midsummer Night's Dream
- Romeo & Juliet
- The Tempest
- Twelfth Night

Further titles in preparation.

The Shakespeare Handbooks

A Guide to
Julius Caesar

by Alistair McCallum

Upstart Crow Publications

*First published in 2017 by
Upstart Crow Publications*

Copyright © Alistair McCallum 2017

All rights reserved

*A CIP catalogue record for this book
is available from the British Library*

ISBN 978 1 899747 11 5

*Printed in Great Britain by Print2demand Ltd,
17 Burgess Road, Ivyhouse Lane, Hastings,
East Sussex TN35 4NR*

www.shakespeare-handbooks.com

Setting the scene

Shakespeare wrote *Julius Caesar* in or around 1599, when he was in his mid-thirties. He was already a successful dramatist and actor, and a member – and shareholder – of the Lord Chamberlain's Men, the most prestigious theatre company in London.

Shakespeare's creative output at this time of his life was prolific and varied: *Much Ado About Nothing, Henry V, Julius Caesar, As You Like It, Hamlet* and *Twelfth Night* were all written within the space of a few years around the turn of the century.

Julius Caesar was undoubtedly one of the first plays presented at the newly-built Globe Theatre in 1599; in fact, some scholars believe that it was written specially for the opening of the new theatre. With its ambitious presentation of a momentous event in history, and its deft movement between public and private scenes, the play was an immediate and continuing success. A few years later, a rival London theatre company, the Admiral's Men, produced a competing play about Caesar, but failed to create the same impact.

The popularity of *Julius Caesar* continued throughout the Restoration, fifty years after Shakespeare's death, when most other plays of the Elizabethan period had come to be regarded as primitive and obscure. It has remained a favourite through the centuries.

Julius Caesar is a play that involves its audience deeply, forcing us to think about character and motive, to weigh opposing arguments, and to confront the contrast between rhetoric and reality. Above all, it is a compelling examination of the power of language:

"There is a powerful ease in the construction of Julius Caesar *which shows us a Shakespeare master of his means, and it is the play in which the boundaries of his art begin so markedly to widen. We find in it, therefore, a stagecraft, not of a too accustomed perfection, but bold and free ... The whole play is alive; it is alive in every line."*

Harley Granville-Barker, *Prefaces to Shakespeare*

Another victory for Caesar

For five years, Rome has been convulsed by civil war. Two factions have been locked in a ferocious struggle for control of the vast, wealthy, ever-expanding Roman Republic.

The dominant group in this conflict is led by Julius Caesar, a populist politician and military hero. Caesar had relentlessly pursued his principal rival, Pompey, as far as Egypt, where he was put to death. After a series of battles, taking place across the Republic, Pompey's sons and remaining supporters were finally hunted down to southern Spain. In the ensuing battle, Caesar has again been victorious.

News of the victory has just reached the city of Rome. The streets are crowded with citizens celebrating Caesar's success and the end of the war, and eagerly hoping for a glimpse of the great man himself as his triumphant procession makes its way through the city.

Curtain up

The celebrations are cut short   I, i

Flavius and Marullus, two government officials, are appalled by the boisterous crowds of people who have gathered in the streets, apparently deserting their workplaces. Flavius addresses them angrily:

> *Flavius:* Hence! home, you idle creatures, get you home:
> Is this a holiday?

The officials are particularly displeased by the fact that those thronging the streets have left behind the tools of their trade and changed out of their workmen's clothes:

> *Flavius:* Speak, what trade art thou?
> *Carpenter:* Why, sir, a carpenter.
> *Marullus:* Where is thy leather apron, and thy rule?
> What dost thou with thy best apparel on?

They question another tradesman, a cobbler, who teases the officials with obscure answers:

> *Marullus:* ... what trade art thou? Answer me directly.
> *Cobbler:* A trade sir, that I hope I may use with a safe conscience;
> which is, indeed, sir, a mender of bad soles.
> *Marullus:* What trade, thou knave? thou naughty[1] knave, what trade?
> *Cobbler:* Nay, I beseech you, sir, be not out[2] with me: yet, if you be
> out,[3] sir, I can mend you.
> *Marullus:* What meanest thou by that?

> [1] *wicked*
> [2] *out of temper; angry*
> [3] *out at heels; having shoes that need mending*

The cobbler eventually comes to the point:

> *Flavius:* Why dost thou lead these men about the streets?
> *Cobbler:* Truly, sir, to wear out their shoes, to get myself into more
> work. But indeed, sir, we make holiday to see Caesar, and
> to rejoice in his triumph.

The officials reprimand the cobbler and his companions sternly. This was not a victory over a foreign power, they assert, but a tragic clash between fellow-Romans; there is no cause for celebration. To make matters worse, the people now rejoicing in the streets did exactly the same for the great general Pompey in the past:

>*Marullus:* Wherefore rejoice? What conquest brings he home?
>   …You blocks, you stones, you worse than senseless things!
>   O you hard hearts, you cruel men of Rome,
>   Knew you not Pompey? Many a time and oft
>   Have you climb'd up to walls and battlements,
>   To towers and windows, yea, to chimney-tops,
>   Your infants in your arms, and there have sat
>   The livelong day, with patient expectation,
>   To see great Pompey pass the streets of Rome …

They should be ashamed of themselves for recklessly celebrating the death of Pompey and his descendants; the only way to make amends, Marullus tells them, is to go home and pray for forgiveness.

Flavius adds that, along with all the others now cheering wildly in the streets, they should weep tears of repentance:

>*Flavius:* Go, go, good countrymen, and for this fault
>   Assemble all the poor men of your sort;
>   Draw them to Tiber banks, and weep your tears
>   Into the channel …

As the crowd quietly disperses, Flavius tells Marullus to remove any decorations that have been hung on statues in Caesar's honour. Marullus is doubtful, and mentions that this is a time of general festivity:

Flavius: Disrobe the images,
      If you find them deck'd with ceremonies.[1]
Marullus: May we do so?
      You know it is the feast of Lupercal.

[1] *decorated with symbols and ornaments*

... it is the feast of Lupercal.

The Lupercalia was a Roman festival of health, purity and fertility, taking place in mid-February. Its origins probably lay in pre-Roman pastoral rituals relating to cleaning and purification, but the Romans associated this time with Lupa, the mythical she-wolf that nursed the infant Romulus and Remus.

One of the traditions of this festival was for young men, wearing only goatskins, to run through the streets of the city carrying whips made from the skin of sacrificed animals. The Greek biographer Plutarch, writing about 150 years after the time of Julius Caesar, describes the ritual, and explains how women would intentionally put themselves in the runners' path:

"... at this time, many noble youths and magistrates would run through the city naked, striking in sport those that they met with leather thongs. And many noblewomen deliberately stood in their way, holding out their hands like schoolchildren to be struck, believing that the pregnant would be helped in delivery, and that those hoping to become pregnant would be helped to conceive."

Flavius dismisses his colleague's concerns, and repeats his instruction. All tokens of celebration must be removed, and any large gatherings of people must be broken up. It is imperative that this hero-worship of Julius Caesar is kept in check; otherwise, there is a danger that Caesar will become all-powerful, threatening the freedom of Roman citizens. He compares Caesar's supporters to the feathers of a menacing young bird of prey:

Flavius: These growing feathers pluck'd from Caesar's wing
Will make him fly an ordinary pitch,[1]
Who else[2] would soar above the view of men
And keep us all in servile fearfulness.

[1] *the height at which a bird of prey flies before swooping on its victim*
[2] *otherwise*

A mysterious warning I, ii

Caesar, accompanied by a group of important politicians and senators, is preparing for the Lupercalian fertility ritual. Mark Antony, Caesar's trusted supporter, is one of the runners in this annual ceremony.

Caesar instructs his wife, Calphurnia, to make sure that she stands in Antony's path when he approaches. Antony, for his part, must take care to touch Calphurnia as he runs past her.

Caesar clearly hopes that strict observance of this time-honoured ritual will help to produce an heir:

Caesar: Forget not, in your speed, Antonius,
To touch Calphurnia; for our elders say,
The barren, touched in this holy chase,
Shake off their sterile curse.
Antony: I shall remember:
When Caesar says, "Do this," it is perform'd.
Caesar: Set on, and leave no ceremony out.

9

Just as they are about to move on, a voice is heard above the shouting and music that surrounds them:

Caesar: Who is it in the press[1] that calls on me?
... Speak. Caesar is turn'd to hear.
Soothsayer: Beware the ides of March.[2]

[1] *tightly-packed crowd*
[2] *mid-point of the month; 15th March*

Caesar is intrigued, and asks two of his companions, the senators Brutus and Cassius, to bring the man before him. However, he quickly loses interest in the fortune-teller, and orders the crowd to stand aside as his group leaves to watch the running:

Caesar: What man is that?
Brutus: A soothsayer bids you beware the ides of March.
Caesar: Set him before me; let me see his face.
Cassius: Fellow, come from the throng; look upon Caesar.
Caesar: What say'st thou to me now? Speak once again.
Soothsayer: Beware the ides of March.
Caesar: He is a dreamer. Let us leave him. Pass.

Rumblings of discontent

Cassius notices that his fellow-senator Brutus is remaining behind while the others leave. Brutus tells his friend to go ahead without him, but Cassius decides to stay, and takes the opportunity to talk candidly with Brutus.

Recently, says Cassius, Brutus has appeared to be distant, even hostile towards him. Brutus apologizes; the truth is that he has been preoccupied with his own conflicting emotions, and as a result has neglected his friends.

Brutus: Cassius,
Be not deceiv'd: if I have veil'd my look,
I turn the trouble of my countenance
Merely upon myself.[1]
... let not therefore my good friends be griev'd
(Among which number, Cassius, be you one)

Nor construe any further my neglect,[2]
Than that poor Brutus, with himself at war,
Forgets the shows of love to other men.

[1] *if I have seemed withdrawn, it is because I am frowning inwardly at myself*
[2] *nor interpret my indifference in any other way*

Cassius accepts that he has been mistaken. This misunderstanding of Brutus's remoteness, he says, has meant that Cassius has kept some important thoughts to himself rather than share them with his friend.

Instead of revealing these thoughts, however, Cassius asks Brutus a question:

Cassius: Tell me, good Brutus, can you see your face?
Brutus: No, Cassius; for the eye sees not itself
But by reflection, by some other things.
Cassius: 'Tis just;
And it is very much lamented, Brutus,
That you have no such mirrors as will turn
Your hidden worthiness into your eye,
That you might see your shadow.[1]

[1] *so that you could see your own hidden qualities*

Cassius says that he is not alone in his admiration; many of the most respected people in Rome – apart from Julius Caesar – have expressed the wish that Brutus might realize his own worth, particularly in these times when freedom is under threat.

Brutus is alarmed; this is dangerous talk. He accuses Cassius of trying to arouse ambitions in him that do not exist:

Brutus: Into what dangers would you lead me, Cassius,
That you would have me seek into myself
For that which is not in me?

Cassius is unrepentant. He is determined, he claims, to make Brutus aware of his own worth and his potential. Brutus would be right to be suspicious if Cassius were insincere, or a flatterer, or a gossip; but Cassius, as his good friend knows, is none of these things.

The conversation is interrupted by the sound of cheering in the distance. Brutus suspects that the crowd has proclaimed Caesar king of Rome. Cassius tentatively asks him to say whether he believes that this is a prospect to be feared.

> The events depicted in *Julius Caesar* took place in 44 BC. At that time Rome was a wealthy, powerful Republic whose lands and provinces included vast swathes of Europe, North Africa and the Middle East. The Republic had been founded hundreds of years before, when Rome was just a small region centred around the city itself. According to legend, Rome had been governed at that time by a series of tyrannical kings, and the Republic had been created with the overthrow of the last of these kings.
>
> Power in the Republic was shared between a number of individuals who usually held their posts for a limited time. Although Republican politics were often violent and chaotic, many Romans held one principle as sacrosanct: that Rome must not return to the days of one-man rule. Caesar, whose military victories had helped him to dominate Roman political life for several years, was regarded as a threat to this principle:
>
> *"It was overweening honours, voted during his lifetime by a compliant senate, combined with his more or less official takeover of the democratic processes that provoked the deadly opposition. He was allowed to wear triumphal dress almost wherever he liked ... Temples and a priesthood in his honour seem to have been promised too, and his statue was placed in all the existing temples of Rome ... Almost worse within the Roman context were the strong hints that he was aiming at becoming a king."*
>
> Mary Beard, *SPQR: A History of Ancient Rome*, 2015

Brutus confirms that, despite his personal friendship with Caesar, he does not want to see Rome governed by an all-powerful individual. Brutus now begins to become impatient with Cassius, and demands to know exactly what is on his mind. He states that his honour – which he values more than his life – will allow him to discuss anything with Cassius as long as it relates to the good of the Republic.

Honour is precisely what he wants to talk about, replies Cassius. He starts by saying that he could never live his life under the dominance of any one individual who, after all, is just a man like himself:

> *Cassius:* I was born free as Caesar; so were you;
> We both have fed as well, and we can both
> Endure the winter's cold as well as he …

Cassius recalls an episode when Caesar challenged him to swim across the Tiber one cold, blustery day. Cassius leapt in without hesitation, and Caesar followed. The two of them fought to cross the stormy water, but Caesar, unable to make it across, cried out for help: Cassius had to rescue him and carry him, exhausted, out of the water. Yet this same man, Cassius claims, now considers himself virtually a god.

Another time, when they were in Spain together, Caesar fell ill. Cassius remembers how he turned pale and shook with fever, and how thin and weak his voice became. This man who wields such superhuman power over others, whose every word is revered, is nothing more than a man, and a weak one at that:

> *Cassius:* Ye gods, it doth amaze me
> A man of such a feeble temper[1] should
> So get the start of[2] the majestic world,
> And bear the palm[3] alone.

> [1] *constitution*
> [2] *gain the advantage over, run ahead of*
> [3] *be victorious (in the contest for power)*

Cassius laments the state of Rome

Cheering is heard once again. Brutus assumes that Caesar, as ever, is the object of the crowd's adulation. His friend's response is bitter and sarcastic:

Brutus: I do believe that these applauses are
For some new honours that are heap'd on Caesar.
Cassius: Why, man, he doth bestride the narrow world
Like a Colossus, and we petty men
Walk under his huge legs, and peep about
To find ourselves dishonourable graves.

Cassius now addresses Brutus directly and purposefully. They and their fellow-Romans have become subservient to Caesar, but this is not their inevitable destiny: they have allowed it to happen, and they can change it.

Cassius: Men at some time are masters of their fates:
The fault, dear Brutus, is not in our stars,
But in ourselves, that we are underlings.

The fault, dear Brutus, is not in our stars ...

"*Cassius has a philosophy that is more Renaissance than Roman, and which, to Shakespeare's original audience, was personified by the imperfectly-known but notorious figure of Niccolò Machiavelli: this is the concept of man as master of his own destiny, independent of any superhuman power ...*"

Norman Sanders, Introduction to the New Penguin edition of *Julius Caesar*, 1967

There is nothing special about the name 'Caesar', says Cassius; the name 'Brutus' is every bit as valid. Indeed, there is nothing special about the man himself. In a passionate outburst, Cassius exclaims that it is shameful that the great Republic of Rome, with its long, proud traditions, has now been reduced to the personal domain of one man:

Cassius: … Upon what meat doth this our Caesar feed,
That he is grown so great? Age, thou art sham'd!
Rome, thou hast lost the breed of noble bloods! [1]
…When could they say, till now, that talk'd of Rome,
That her wide walks encompass'd but [2] one man?

[1] *noble families; people of honourable character*
[2] *only*

Cassius reminds Brutus of his famous ancestor, Lucius Junius Brutus; centuries ago, he had led a revolt against the tyrannical regime of the king of Rome, abolished one-man rule, and founded the Republic:

Cassius: O, you and I have heard our fathers say,
There was a Brutus once that would have brook'd
Th'eternal devil to keep his state in Rome
As easily as a king.[1]

[1] *who would have tolerated the devil as ruler of Rome as soon as a king*

Confronted with this powerful rhetoric, Brutus remains cautious. He does not doubt his friend's love, he assures him, and understands his reasoning. He intends to discuss his own views with Cassius when the time is right; for the present, however, Brutus needs time to consider, and wishes to keep his thoughts to himself.

Brutus asks Cassius not to pursue the subject any further at the moment, but makes it clear where his sympathies lie:

> *Brutus:* ... Brutus had rather be a villager [1]
> Than to repute himself a son of Rome
> Under these hard conditions as this time
> Is like [2] to lay upon us.
>
> [1] *a peasant of no standing (rather than a proud citizen of Rome)*
> [2] *likely*

At this point Caesar, surrounded by his followers, returns from the Lupercalian ceremonies. As the entourage approaches, Cassius tells Brutus to attract the attention of the senator Casca, so that they can ask him for the latest news.

However, it quickly becomes clear that there is an uneasy atmosphere around Caesar. He himself looks displeased, and his wife is pale. His followers seem quiet and fearful, and the senator Cicero looks angry and resentful.

> *"The telling comparisons between Brutus and Caesar demonstrate the play's most essential ambivalence: the tyrant and his opponent are not easily distinguishable ... Both Brutus and Caesar have great leadership qualities, and, being certain of his virtues, each is susceptible to flattery and manipulation by lesser men."*
>
> Charles Boyce, *Shakespeare A to Z*, 1990

Caesar distrusts Cassius

Caesar notices Cassius nearby, and remarks to Antony that he is suspicious of intense, austere men of his kind:

Caesar: Let me have men about me that are fat,
Sleek-headed[1] men, and such as sleep a-nights.
Yond Cassius has a lean and hungry look;
He thinks too much: such men are dangerous.

[1] *well-groomed*

Antony assures Caesar that Cassius is good-natured and trustworthy, but Caesar is adamant:

Caesar: He reads much,
He is a great observer, and he looks
Quite through the deeds of men.[1] He loves no plays,
As thou dost, Antony; he hears no music.
Seldom he smiles, and smiles in such a sort[2]
As if he mock'd himself …

[1] *sees men's motives with complete clarity*
[2] *manner*

In short, says Caesar, Cassius is not to be trusted. People like him are always liable to be envious of those greater than themselves, and are potentially dangerous. However, Caesar is at pains to point out that he himself is not fearful:

Caesar: I rather tell thee what is to be fear'd
Than what I fear; for always I am Caesar.

Caesar is determined to question Antony further about Cassius, and the two men continue their conversation as they leave.

An eye-witness account

Brutus and Cassius again remain behind as Caesar moves on with his group of followers. Now, however, Casca joins them, prompted by Brutus, who had pulled secretively at his cloak as he passed by. Casca reveals the reason for the cheering they heard earlier. As Brutus had suspected, Caesar was the object of the crowd's appreciation:

> Casca: ... there was a crown offer'd him; and, being offer'd him, he put it by[1] with the back of his hand, thus; and then the people fell a-shouting.
>
> [1] *pushed it aside*

This scene was acted out three times, says Casca, Antony being the one offering Caesar the crown. Casca describes the episode scornfully, claiming that he was hardly taking any notice of events:

> Casca: I can as well be hang'd as tell the manner of it: it was mere foolery; I did not mark it.[1] I saw Mark Antony offer him a crown ... and, as I told you, he put it by once; but for all that, to my thinking, he would fain[2] have had it. Then he offered it to him again ...
>
> [1] *it was complete nonsense, and I didn't pay any attention to it*
> [2] *willingly*

After refusing the crown for a third time, reports Casca, Caesar fell, unconscious, to the ground. Cassius is startled; but Brutus, a close friend of Caesar's, is aware that he suffers from a condition known as the falling-sickness, resulting in occasional fits. Cassius remarks bitterly that is the citizens of Rome who are afflicted rather than Caesar, but his comment is lost on the plain-spoken Casca:

> Cassius: ... what, did Caesar swound?[1]
> Casca: He fell down in the market-place, and foam'd at mouth, and was speechless.
> Brutus: 'Tis very like;[2] he hath the falling-sickness.

18

Cassius: No, Caesar hath it not; but you, and I,
And honest Casca, we have the falling-sickness.
Casca: I know not what you mean by that, but I am sure Caesar fell down.

[1] *faint*
[2] *likely*

What really struck Casca, however, was not Caesar's fainting but the behaviour of the crowd. Like an audience at a melodramatic play, they went wild with excitement when Caesar refused the crown that was offered to him; and when he recovered from his fainting fit, and asked the people for their forgiveness, they again cheered riotously.

Are the conspirators right to fear Caesar's ambitions? Did Shakespeare side with the conspirators or with Caesar? And how should we view the conspiracy? Different directors, actors and audiences may have different opinions, but the play itself does not provide straightforward answers:

"*Modern productions have attempted to stabilize the play's political sympathies through topical costuming – the conspirators as freedom fighters against a dictatorship, or the patricians as the self-interested fat cats of an undemocratic state – but in Shakespeare's hands the balance of sympathies is more delicate. Does Caesar have absolutist aspirations to disband the republic and accept the crown? We don't know, because the scene is only reported, not shown.*"

Laurie Maguire and Emma Smith, *30 Great Myths about Shakespeare*, 2013

Casca is contemptuous of the common people of Rome, and the way in which Caesar manipulates them:

> *Casca:* Three or four wenches, where I stood, cried, "Alas, good soul," and forgave him with all their hearts; but there's no heed to be taken of them; if Caesar stabb'd their mothers, they would have done no less.

However, Caesar was clearly troubled by the fact that he had fainted in public, and this accounted for the tense atmosphere around him as he returned from the Lupercalian ceremonies.

Cassius asks how the senator Cicero reacted to these events. Casca confirms that he heard an enigmatic remark from the famously well-educated Cicero, but was none the wiser:

> *Cassius:* Did Cicero say anything?
> *Casca:* Ay, he spoke Greek.
> *Cassius:* To what effect?[1]
> *Casca:* Nay, and I tell you that, I'll ne'er look you i' th' face again.[2] But those that understood him smil'd at one another, and shook their heads; but for mine own part, it was Greek to me.[3]
>
> [1] *to what purpose, with what meaning*
> [2] *if I claimed to tell you, I would be dishonest*
> [3] *I couldn't understand a word of it*

Casca adds a chilling footnote: without giving details, he hints that harsh punishment has been meted out to the two officials who earlier ordered the removal of decorations that had been hung on statues in Caesar's honour.

> *Casca:* ... Marullus and Flavius, for pulling scarfs off Caesar's images, are put to silence.[1]
>
> [1] *removed from their positions; possibly, exiled or even executed*

Cassius and Casca agree to meet for dinner tomorrow. After Casca has left, Brutus remarks on the bluntness of his character. Cassius replies that his abrupt, sardonic manner hides an astute mind:

> *Cassius:* ... This rudeness is a sauce to his good wit,
> Which gives men stomach to digest his words
> With better appetite.

Brutus now leaves. He too will meet Cassius tomorrow, so that they can continue their discussion.

Alone, Cassius reflects on Brutus's character. Despite his nobility, believes Cassius, he is susceptible to influence. And Cassius knows that, unlike himself, Brutus is a trusted friend of Caesar's; he will be a useful ally.

Cassius has already established that Brutus is unhappy about the way things are going in Rome. To strengthen his resolve, Cassius intends to forge some letters and leave them, anonymously, in Brutus's house. While they will appear to come from different people, they will all emphasize the high regard in which Brutus is held, and hint at the danger posed by Caesar's hunger for power. If his stratagem succeeds, declares Cassius, Caesar will need to be vigilant:

> *Cassius:* I will this night,
> In several hands, in at his windows throw,
> As if they came from several citizens,
> Writings, all tending to the great opinion
> That Rome holds of his name; wherein obscurely
> Caesar's ambition shall be glanced at.
> And after this, let Caesar seat him sure,[1]
> For we will shake him, or worse days endure.
>
> [1] *make himself secure*

A sense of foreboding   I, iii

It is late at night, and a violent storm is sweeping through the streets of Rome. Cicero comes across Casca, who is terrified; this is by far the worst storm he has ever witnessed. The earth itself is shaking, and fire seems to be falling from the sky. Casca fears that the tempest is a sign of the gods' anger, and he is amazed at Cicero's calmness:

> *Casca:* Are you not mov'd, when all the sway[1] of earth
> Shakes like a thing unfirm?
> ... never till to-night, never till now,
> Did I go through a tempest dropping fire.
> Either there is a civil strife in heaven,
> Or else the world, too saucy[2] with the gods,
> Incenses them to send destruction.
>
> [1] *realm*
> [2] *insolent, disrespectful*

Casca describes some other strange, ominous events that he has seen or heard about lately: a man whose hand inexplicably burst into flames and burned brightly, even though it caused him no pain; a lion prowling around the centre of Rome; a group of women huddled in fear, having seen men whose bodies were blazing with fire wandering through the streets; and a screech-owl, a sinister bird of the night, shrieking in the market-place at midday.

"*These monstrous and unnatural happenings in the natural world were easily related by the Elizabethans both to man's inner life and to society itself, owing to the infinite series of interlocking correspondences which they perceived between the personal, social, material, and universal levels of life.*"

Norman Sanders, Introduction to the New Penguin edition of *Julius Caesar*, 1967

Incidents like these, all happening around the same time, cannot be explained away as natural phenomena, claims Casca; there must be a profound significance behind them. Cicero warns him that attempts to find meaning in such events may be misguided:

> *Cicero:* Indeed, it is a strange-disposed time: [1]
> But men may construe things, after their fashion, [2]
> Clean from [3] the purpose of the things themselves.
>
> [1] *a time when strange things are likely to happen*
> [2] *may interpret events to suit their own ideas*
> [3] *in a way that bears no relation to*

Cicero asks Casca whether Caesar will be at the Capitol (the political centre of Rome, where the senate-house is located) tomorrow. Casca confirms that he will be there, and Cicero goes on his way.

Casca is persuaded

Just as Cicero leaves, another voice is heard in the darkness. It is Cassius. Unlike Casca, he is not afraid of the storm; in fact, he is relishing it.

> *Cassius:* For my part, I have walk'd about the streets,
> Submitting me unto the perilous night ...
> And when the cross [1] blue lightning seem'd to open
> The breast of heaven, I did present myself
> Even in the aim and very flash of it. [2]
>
> [1] *forked, branching*
> [2] *exactly at the point where I thought the lightning might strike*

Casca is horrified; a dangerous storm like this, brought on by the anger of the gods, should fill him with dread and humility. Cassius tells him impatiently that he has completely misunderstood the storm and the other omens that have been reported in recent days. These are important signs which should be welcomed, not feared:

>*Cassius:* You are dull, Casca, and those sparks of life
> That should be in a Roman you do want,
> Or else you use not.[1] You look pale, and gaze,
> And put on[2] fear, and cast yourself in wonder,[3]
> To see the strange impatience of the heavens ...
>
> [1] *you are without them, or you are neglecting them*
> [2] *display*
> [3] *throw yourself into a state of wonder*

This disorder in nature, explains Cassius, should be seen as a timely warning of disorder in the Republic itself. He draws a parallel between recent ominous events and the unnatural dominance of one man over Rome. He does not need to name the man:

>*Cassius:* Now could I, Casca, name to thee a man
> Most like this dreadful night,
> That thunders, lightens, opens graves, and roars
> As doth the lion in the Capitol;
> A man no mightier than thyself, or me,
> In personal action, yet prodigious[1] grown,
> And fearful, as these strange eruptions are.[2]
>*Casca:* 'Tis Caesar that you mean, is it not, Cassius?
>*Cassius:* Let it be who it is ...
>*Casca:* Indeed, they say the senators to-morrow
> Mean to establish Caesar as a king ...
>
> [1] *threatening, ill-omened*
> [2] *frightening, just like the recent disturbances in nature*

But there is an answer to despotism, says Cassius, indicating his dagger: even if all his other freedoms are taken away, he will always be free to shake off the burden of tyranny by taking his own life. He does not even blame Caesar; it is the apathetic, weak-spirited Romans themselves, Cassius claims, who are responsible for Rome's decline.

> *Cassius:* ... why should Caesar be a tyrant then?
> Poor man! I know he would not [1] be a wolf,
> But that [2] he sees the Romans are but sheep;
> He were [3] no lion, were not Romans hinds.
>
> [1] *would not wish to be*
> [2] *were it not for the fact that*
> [3] *would be*

At the height of his emotional outburst, Cassius suddenly breaks off. Perhaps Casca disagrees; perhaps he is a willing participant in his own oppression? If so, Cassius accepts that his words may get him into serious trouble, but he is unconcerned for his own safety. At this point, Casca declares passionately that he supports Cassius, and will take a leading part in any action that he chooses to organize:

> *Casca:* ... Be factious [1] for redress of all these griefs,[2]
> And I will set this foot of mine as far
> As who goes furthest.
>
> [1] *form a group of like-minded people*
> [2] *grievances*

As they clasp hands, Cassius reveals that such a plan is already under way, involving some of the most honourable men in Rome. In fact, his accomplices are expecting to meet him this very night. They are gathering outdoors, under the shelter of a large portico; it should be safe to meet tonight, as the combination of strange, supernatural events and wild weather means that the streets are empty.

Cassius finally hints at the precise nature of his plan:

> *Cassius:* ... this fearful night,
> There is no stir or walking in the streets;
> And the complexion of the element
> In favour's like the work we have in hand,[1]
> Most bloody, fiery, and most terrible.
>
> [1] *the condition of the sky is similar, in its appearance, to the scheme we have undertaken*

A figure suddenly emerges through the storm. It is Cinna, another of the conspirators against Caesar. He has been looking for Cassius, who is expected at the planned gathering under the portico.

Cinna is glad to hear that Casca has joined the plot, but the real prize would be to have Brutus on their side. Cassius tells him not to worry, and gives him some letters to distribute in certain places where Brutus will find them. When that has been done, they are all to meet as planned. The names of the various conspirators now come to light: Cassius, Casca and Cinna will be joined in their scheme by Trebonius, Decius Brutus and Metellus Cimber.

The conspirators will be visiting Brutus later tonight, Cassius tells Casca, and he is convinced that they will be able to win him over wholeheartedly to their cause. Casca, like Cinna, realizes how valuable Brutus's involvement would be:

> *Casca:* O, he sits high in all the people's hearts:
> And that which would appear offence in us,
> His countenance,[1] like richest alchemy,
> Will change to virtue and to worthiness.
>
> [1] *approval, support*

A fateful decision II, i

Brutus, unable to sleep, is outside in his garden, gazing at the stars. He calls impatiently for his servant, and instructs him to light a candle in his study. When Brutus is alone again, it immediately becomes clear that he has been agonizing over the fate of Caesar and the future of Rome.

> *Brutus:* It must be by his death: and for my part,
> I know no personal cause to spurn at[1] him,
> But for the general.[2] He would be[3] crown'd:
> How that might change his nature, there's the question.
>
> [1] *attack*
> [2] *for the people; for the general good*
> [3] *wishes to be*

Dawn is not far off, and Brutus remarks that it is in bright sunlight that dangerous snakes emerge. If Caesar is crowned, becoming the sole ruler of Rome, he too will become a threat, and will be able to act with impunity. Absolute power can lead to terrible cruelty:

> *Brutus:* It is the bright day that brings forth the adder,
> And that craves[1] wary walking. Crown him; – that;
> And then, I grant, we put a sting in him,
> That at his will he may do danger with.
> Th' abuse of greatness is when it disjoins
> Remorse from power[2] …
>
> [1] *demands, calls for*
> [2] *when it separates compassion from power*

Brutus, who knows Caesar well, accepts that he is a rational man, and not inclined to act capriciously. However, reflects Brutus, a calm, restrained demeanour can hide ruthless ambition; and if Caesar becomes all-powerful, a very different character may well emerge. This must be prevented, he decides.

Given Caesar's undoubted popularity, however, it will not be easy to justify his death. Brutus runs through, in his mind, how the decision might best be presented:

Brutus: Fashion[1] it thus: that what he is, augmented,
Would run to these and these extremities;[2]
And therefore think him as a serpent's egg,
Which, hatch'd, would, as his kind, grow mischievous,[3]
And kill him in the shell.

[1] *shape, depict*
[2] *his ambitious character, if allowed to develop, would lead to various examples of cruelty*
[3] *would, as is its nature, become evil and harmful*

Shakespeare's soliloquies – complex, introspective monologues in which a character's thoughts and feelings are explored – are among his most famous speeches. There are numerous examples in later plays such as *Hamlet* and *Macbeth*: however, it is in *Julius Caesar*, in the scene in Brutus's garden, that Shakespeare's first serious exploration of the soliloquy occurs. In fact, this seems to have been an exceptionally prolific, inventive period in Shakespeare's career:

"Something extraordinary was beginning to happen as Shakespeare wrote Julius Caesar *in the spring of 1599. The various strands of politics, character, inwardness, contemporary events, even Shakespeare's own reflections on the act of writing, began to infuse each other ... the streamlined* Julius Caesar *feels as if it was written without interruption in a few short weeks."*

James Shapiro, *1599: A Year in the Life of William Shakespeare*, 2005

Brutus's servant Lucius returns, having lit a candle in his study as instructed. Lucius mentions that he has just found a letter in the room, and hands it over to Brutus.

Just as his servant is about to return to bed, it occurs to Brutus that the approaching day may be the ides of March, mentioned by the soothsayer on the day of the Lupercalia. He sends his servant away to check the calendar, and reads the letter. Although it is dark in the garden, a meteor shower – another strange phenomenon in this time of ominous events – provides enough light to read by.

The letter is short and urgent, but puzzling:

> *Brutus, thou sleep'st; awake, and see thyself.*
> *Shall Rome, etc. Speak, strike, redress!*

Brutus tries to make sense of the note which, he remarks, is not the first of its kind that he has received recently. In trying to guess at the writer's intentions, he remembers his renowned forefather, who had expelled the last king of Rome, the despotic Tarquin:

> *Brutus:* "Shall Rome, etc." Thus must I piece it out: [1]
> Shall Rome stand under one man's awe? [2] What, Rome?
> My ancestors did from the streets of Rome
> The Tarquin drive, when he was call'd a king.
>
> [1] *complete the sentence, develop the meaning*
> [2] *oppression, intimidation*

Brutus is now more determined than ever to strike against Caesar. His servant Lucius returns, and confirms that the coming day is indeed the ides of March. At the same time, knocking at the gate is heard, and Lucius leaves once more to deal with the visitors.

It now becomes clear how agitated Brutus is. In fact, he has been in mental turmoil since the conversation with Cassius at the time of the Lupercalia. In this period between the initial idea of removing Caesar and the act itself, Brutus is suffering a terrible inner conflict:

> Brutus: Since Cassius first did whet[1] me against Caesar,
> I have not slept.
> Between the acting of a dreadful thing
> And the first motion,[2] all the interim is
> Like a phantasma,[3] or a hideous dream ...
> ... the state of man,
> Like to a little kingdom, suffers then
> The nature of an insurrection.
>
> [1] *sharpen; arouse*
> [2] *impulse, prompting*
> [3] *hallucination*

The conspirators meet

Lucius announces that Cassius is at the gate. There are others with him, but their faces are half-hidden in their clothing, and Lucius does not recognize them.

Brutus realizes that these are the conspirators, and he tells his servant to let them in. If they feel it is necessary to conceal themselves even at night, wonders Brutus, how will they remain hidden in broad daylight? The only answer is to disguise their intentions under a friendly exterior:

> Brutus: They are the faction.[1] O conspiracy,
> Sham'st thou to show thy dangerous brow by night,
> When evils are most free? O, then by day
> Where wilt thou find a cavern dark enough
> To mask thy monstrous[2] visage? Seek none, conspiracy;
> Hide it in smiles and affability ...
>
> [1] *the group plotting against Caesar*
> [2] *unnatural, hideous*

The visitors join Brutus in the darkness of the garden. Led by Cassius, the group of conspirators consists of Casca, Decius Brutus, Cinna, Metellus Cimber, and Trebonius. They are all known to Brutus, and Cassius assures him that they all hold him in high esteem.

Cassius takes Brutus aside briefly to discuss the plot, and the remaining conspirators look around anxiously for signs of daybreak. When the two return, Brutus asks each man for his hand. Cassius proposes that they swear an oath, but Brutus overrules him. He insists, passionately, that the word of a Roman, in a noble cause, and between honourable companions, is enough:

> *Brutus:* ... What need we any spur but our own cause
> To prick[1] us to redress? What other bond
> Than secret[2] Romans, that have spoke the word,
> And will not palter?[3] And what other oath
> Than honesty to honesty engag'd,[4]
> That this shall be, or we will fall for it?
>
> [1] *incite, urge*
> [2] *discreet, able to keep a secret*
> [3] *quibble, hesitate*
> [4] *exchanged words of honour*

Cassius raises a question: what about Cicero? He is likely to agree with their cause, and would be a valuable accomplice. Metellus points out that his age and experience would lend gravity to their undertaking; if he supported them, they would not be accused of youthful impulsiveness. However, Brutus disagrees, believing that Cicero would never agree to a scheme that he had not initiated himself.

Final resolutions

Another question now arises. Decius Brutus, without naming the deed, asks whether there should be more than one victim:

Decius: Shall no man else be touch'd but only Caesar?
Cassius: Decius, well urg'd. I think it is not meet,[1]
Mark Antony, so well belov'd of Caesar,
Should outlive Caesar ...

[1] *right, fitting*

Julius Caesar was written at a time of great political tension in England. One question, which had been simmering for many years, was becoming increasingly urgent, even if it could not be discussed in public: who should succeed the childless Queen Elizabeth, now in her sixties? There were various rival claimants, and speculation was rife about the views of influential courtiers such as the ambitious Earl of Essex.

In this febrile atmosphere, the authorities were becoming uncomfortable with any depictions of English history in print or on the stage:

"The censorship of the stage exercised by court officialdom meant that it was exceedingly risky to dramatize contemporary affairs, so the best way of writing political drama was to take subjects from the past and leave it to the audience to see the parallel in the present. The uncertainty over the succession to the Virgin Queen meant that there were frequent whispers of conspiracy in the final years of Elizabeth's reign. It would hardly have been appropriate to write a play about a group of highly placed courtiers – the Earl of Essex and his circle, say – plotting to overthrow the monarchy. But a play about a group of highly placed Roman patricians – Brutus, Cassius and company – plotting to assassinate Julius Caesar had the capacity to raise some awkward questions by means of the implicit parallel."

Jonathan Bate, *Soul of the Age*, 2009

Cassius is convinced that Antony, if allowed to live, would seek revenge; he is astute and resourceful, and would pose a continual threat to them all. Again, Brutus overrules him:

> *Brutus:* Our course will seem too bloody, Caius Cassius,
> To cut the head off and then hack the limbs,
> Like wrath in death and envy afterwards;
> For Antony is but a limb of Caesar.
> Let's be sacrificers, but not butchers …

The killing of Caesar must be seen as a sad necessity, insists Brutus. It is not to be carried out in a spirit of anger or resentment. They are acting for the general good, not out of malice, and it is essential that this is made clear to the people of Rome:

> *Brutus:* … gentle friends,
> Let's kill him boldly, but not wrathfully;
> Let's carve him as a dish fit for the gods,
> Not hew[1] him as a carcass fit for hounds.
> … This shall make
> Our purpose necessary, and not envious;[2]
> Which so appearing to the common eyes,
> We shall be call'd purgers,[3] not murderers.
>
> [1] *hack*
> [2] *this will make our plan seem necessary, and not spiteful*
> [3] *healers*

Cassius protests, but Brutus is adamant that Antony's life should be spared. Antony will undoubtedly grieve at Caesar's death, but the worst that he can do is become melancholy, and perhaps even take his own life. This outcome is unlikely, claims Brutus, given Antony's well-known love of pleasure and company.

The discussion is interrupted by the sound of a clock striking. It is three in the morning, and the gathering now starts to break up. Cassius, however, has another point to make:

Brutus: Peace! Count the clock.
Cassius: The clock hath stricken three.
Trebonius: 'Tis time to part.
Cassius: But it is doubtful yet
Whether Caesar will come forth to-day or no;
For he is superstitious grown of late ...

The famously sceptical Caesar, Cassius suspects, is becoming interested in dreams, omens and such things. The recent spate of strange phenomena, along with warnings from clairvoyants, may persuade him to stay at home rather than risk going to the Capitol.

The clock hath stricken three.

This line is often mentioned as an example of Shakespeare's anachronisms; striking clocks did not exist in Ancient Rome. Several other examples can be found in *Julius Caesar*, and throughout Shakespeare's work. However, it would be misguided to imagine that these arose from carelessness or ignorance. The idea of achieving strict historical accuracy would simply have been meaningless to a playwright of the time.

In the original productions, there would have been little or no attempt to reproduce the physical conditions of Ancient Rome in the stage sets, or in the actors' costumes or language. All Shakespeare's plays, regardless of their setting in time or place, are firmly rooted in his own culture. Part of that culture, of course, was the Bible, and this line would have reminded the audience that, just as Peter would inevitably betray Jesus, so Brutus will betray his friend Caesar:

Jesus said unto Peter, Verily I say unto thee, That this night, before the cock crow, thou shalt deny me thrice.

Gospel of St. Matthew, King James Bible, 1611

Decius is confident that he can talk Caesar out of any doubts he may have about leaving his house on the ides of March. Cassius, however, decides that they should all meet Caesar, at eight o'clock this morning, and accompany him to the Capitol.

Metellus Cimber suddenly thinks of another man who would willingly join their conspiracy. His name is Caius Ligarius, and he is known to hold a grudge against Caesar, who reprimanded him for praising Caesar's old enemy Pompey. Brutus asks Metellus to find Ligarius; the man is a friend of his, and it should not be difficult to win him over.

Dawn is finally breaking, and the conspirators leave. As they go, Cassius urges them to bear in mind that they have given their word to go through with this undertaking. Brutus, in contrast, encourages them to present a positive face to the outside world:

> *Cassius:* ... all remember
> What you have said, and show yourselves true Romans.
> *Brutus:* Good gentlemen, look fresh and merrily.
> Let not our looks put on our purposes,[1]
> But bear it as our Roman actors do,
> With untir'd[2] spirits and formal constancy.[3]
> And so good morrow to you every one.
>
> [1] *betray our intentions*
> [2] *alert; undisguised, open*
> [3] *your customary dignified composure*

Now alone, Brutus calls out for his servant once more. He then realizes that Lucius, unlike himself, is enjoying the benefits of sleep, and decides not to disturb him:

> *Brutus:* Boy! Lucius! Fast asleep? It is no matter;
> Enjoy the honey-heavy dew of slumber:
> Thou hast no figures nor no fantasies[1]
> Which busy care[2] draws in the brains of men;
> Therefore thou sleep'st so sound.
>
> [1] *imagined forms or images*
> [2] *continual anxiety*

Brutus's wife demands an explanation

Brutus is startled by a voice in the garden. He is shocked to find that his wife, Portia, has come out into the cold early morning air. She is concerned about his strange, restless behaviour, and is upset that he refuses to confide in her:

> *Portia:*　　　　　　Y'have ungently, Brutus,
> Stole[1] from my bed; and yesternight at supper
> You suddenly arose, and walk'd about,
> Musing, and sighing, with your arms across;[2]
> And when I ask'd you what the matter was,
> You star'd upon me with ungentle looks.
> I urg'd you further; then you scratch'd your head,
> And too impatiently stamp'd with your foot;
> Yet[3] I insisted, yet you answer'd not ...
>
> [1] *crept silently*
> [2] *crossed*
> [3] *still, repeatedly*

Brutus claims that he is ill, but Portia refuses to believe that this lies behind his troubled state of mind. If he were unwell, he would not be spending time in the raw, damp night air:

> *Portia:*　Is Brutus sick, and is it physical[1]
> To walk unbraced[2] and suck up the humours[3]
> Of the dank morning?
> 　　　　　　　　　　... No, my Brutus;
> You have some sick offence[4] within your mind,
> Which, by the right and virtue of my place,
> I ought to know of ...
>
> [1] *healing, restorative*
> [2] *with clothes unfastened, not warmly dressed*
> [3] *damp, unhealthy vapours*
> [4] *harmful disturbance*

Eventually she resorts to kneeling in front of Brutus, pleading with him to share his worries. She is also aware that several mysterious, secretive visitors have called on Brutus.

Portia complains that it is cruel and insulting of Brutus to exclude her from his innermost life in this way:

> *Portia:* Am I your self
> But, as it were, in sort or limitation,[1]
> To keep with you at meals, comfort your bed,
> And talk to you sometimes? Dwell I but [2] in the suburbs
> Of your good pleasure? If it be no more,
> Portia is Brutus' harlot, not his wife.
>
> [1] *part of you in a limited way, or only for a specified time*
> [2] *only*

Brutus assures Portia that he loves her and holds her in the highest regard, but she refuses to be appeased. She is trustworthy, she insists, and he can safely share his secrets with her; indeed, her late father Cato was one of the most respected statesmen in Rome.

Dwell I but in the suburbs
Of your good pleasure?

In Shakespeare's day, the 'suburbs' referred to the areas of London outside the control of the city authorities. The landowners of these areas were generally fairly tolerant, and the suburbs – just a short walk from the city centre – were notorious for activities such as prostitution and bear-baiting. Most theatres (including the Globe, where *Julius Caesar* was first performed) were in the suburbs; suspicions about their propriety, and the noisy crowds of people who attended plays, made them unpopular both with the puritanical city authorities and with local residents of more respectable areas. It was to be several years before Shakespeare's theatre company managed to set up a second theatre in a wealthier, more salubrious location.

"Portia's observation that the harlot metaphorically dwells in the suburbs of a man's life alludes to the actual dwelling places of prostitutes in London's suburbs."

Alison Findlay, *Women in Shakespeare*, 2014

To Brutus's astonishment, she dramatically reveals a wound that she has inflicted on herself:

>*Portia:* I have made strong proof of my constancy,[1]
>Giving myself a voluntary wound
>Here, in the thigh: can I bear that with patience,
>And not my husband's secrets?
>*Brutus:* O ye gods,
>Render me worthy of this noble wife!

[1] *a severe trial of my steadfastness*

Knocking is heard at the gate once more. Promising Portia that he will soon reveal everything to her, he asks her to go indoors.

Another conspirator is recruited

The visitor is Caius Ligarius, earlier recommended by Metellus Cimber as a potential supporter of their cause.

Brutus is dismayed to find that Ligarius is ill. However, Ligarius, although he does not know exactly what Brutus has planned, insists that he is fit to take part in any honourable enterprise. When Brutus mentions that he does indeed have an important scheme in hand, Ligarius is enthusiastic despite his illness.

Brutus hints that the action he has in mind is necessary for the health of the Roman Republic. Although no names are mentioned, Ligarius, a great admirer of Brutus and his famous ancestor, makes it clear that he understands exactly what Brutus means:

>*Ligarius:* Soul of Rome!
>Brave son, deriv'd from honourable loins!
>Thou, like an exorcist, hast conjur'd up
>My mortified spirit.[1] Now bid me run,
>And I will strive with things impossible,
>Yea, get the better of them. What's to do?
>*Brutus:* A piece of work that will make sick men whole.[2]
>*Ligarius:* But are not some whole that we must make sick?

> *Brutus:* That must we also. What it is, my Caius,
> I shall unfold to thee …
>
> [1] *raised my lifeless spirit*
> [2] *healthy, wholesome*

The time has come for the plan to be put into action, says Brutus. He leads the way out of the garden, and Ligarius follows willingly.

Calphurnia is adamant II, ii

The scene moves to Caesar's house. Caesar, still in his nightgown, complains that he has had a disturbed night; as well as the strange, violent storm, he has heard his wife Calphurnia crying out in her sleep, screaming that Caesar's life is in danger.

Caesar calls for a servant, and orders him to pass on a command to his priests; they are to carry out an animal sacrifice immediately, and let him know whether the resulting omens are favourable or not.

Calphurnia now joins her husband. She is appalled that he is even thinking of leaving home today. She has been profoundly shaken by the unnatural recent events. As well as the things she has witnessed herself, she has heard frightening reports from her attendants:

> *Calphurnia:* Caesar, I never stood on ceremonies,[1]
> Yet now they fright me. There is one within,[2]
> Besides the things that we have heard and seen,
> Recounts most horrid sights seen by the watch.[3]
> A lioness hath whelp'd[4] in the streets,
> And graves have yawn'd and yielded up their dead;
> Fierce fiery warriors fight upon the clouds …
>
> [1] *attached importance to omens*
> [2] *someone in the house*
> [3] *night watchmen*
> [4] *given birth*

Caesar replies that, regardless of these portents, he intends to go to the Capitol. Whatever destiny has in store, it cannot be avoided; besides, these strange signs are visible to all, and are not aimed at one man. Calphurnia disagrees, believing that their sinister message is for those in power, but Caesar refuses to be ruled by fear:

Calphurnia: When beggars die, there are no comets seen;
　　　　　　The heavens themselves blaze forth the death of princes.
Caesar:　　Cowards die many times before their deaths;
　　　　　　The valiant never taste of death but once.
　　　　　　Of all the wonders that I yet have heard,
　　　　　　It seems to me most strange that men should fear,
　　　　　　Seeing that death, a necessary end,
　　　　　　Will come when it will come.

Caesar's servant now returns. The news from the priests is not good: they have sacrificed an animal, and discovered that it had no heart. Caesar should not leave his house today, they warn.

In the 1970s, a copy of the complete works of Shakespeare was smuggled into the prison on South Africa's Robben Island, which held many political prisoners during the Apartheid era. The book, which became known as the 'Robben Island Bible', was passed around secretly from cell to cell, and many prisoners underlined passages in the text that they found particularly significant.

Nelson Mandela, imprisoned on the island for eighteen years, selected a speech from *Julius Caesar*:

Cowards die many times before their deaths;
The valiant never taste of death but once.

40

However, Caesar sees this as a challenge, and it makes him even more determined to set out for the Capitol:

Caesar: The gods do this in shame of cowardice:[1]
Caesar should be a beast without a heart
If he should stay at home today for[2] fear.
No, Caesar shall not. Danger knows full well
That Caesar is more dangerous than he.

[1] *to put cowardice to shame*
[2] *out of*

Calphurnia again implores him to stay at home. He can blame it on her fearfulness, she suggests, rather than any anxiety of his own. His friend Mark Antony can pass a message to the other senators that Caesar is ill. In desperation, she kneels before him, and he finally agrees; for her sake, he will remain at home today.

A change of heart

At this moment, the conspirator Decius Brutus arrives to greet Caesar. He has come to accompany Caesar to the Capitol for today's meeting of the Senate.

Caesar tells his visitor that he has decided not to go to the Capitol today. Despite his earlier discussion with his wife, he refuses to be seen as openly deceitful. As a renowned military leader, he does not need to make excuses, he declares impatiently:

Caesar: … tell them that I will not come to-day:
Cannot, is false; and that I dare not, falser;
I will not come to-day. Tell them so, Decius.
Calphurnia: Say he is sick.
Caesar: Shall Caesar send a lie?
Have I in conquest stretch'd mine arm so far,
To be afeard to tell greybeards[1] the truth?
Decius, go tell them Caesar will not come.
Decius: Most mighty Caesar, let me know some cause,
Lest I be laugh'd at when I tell them so.
Caesar: The cause is in my will: I will not come;
That is enough to satisfy the Senate.

[1] *the old men of the Senate*

41

Relenting a little, Caesar agrees to reveal to Decius the true reason for his decision. Decius is a close friend, and Caesar tells him, confidentially, that he is remaining at home at the insistence of his wife Calphurnia, who had a frightening dream last night:

Caesar: She dreamt to-night she saw my statue,
Which like a fountain with an hundred spouts
Did run pure blood; and many lusty[1] Romans
Came smiling, and did bathe their hands in it.
And these she does apply for[2] warnings and portents
And evils imminent ...

[1] *eager, lively*
[2] *she interprets these images as*

She was so shaken by the dream, says Caesar, that she begged him to stay away from the Senate; and for her sake, he has agreed.

Thinking quickly, Decius explains that his wife's interpretation of her dream is mistaken. Far from representing death, the blood of her dream signifies the fresh life and renewal that Caesar will bring to Rome and its fortunate inhabitants. Decius then alleges that there is a good reason why Caesar should attend the Senate today:

Decius: The Senate have concluded
To give this day a crown to mighty Caesar.
If you shall send them word you will not come,
Their minds may change. Besides, it were a mock
Apt to be render'd,[1] for some one to say,
"Break up the Senate till another time,
When Caesar's wife shall meet with better dreams."

[1] *a sarcastic comment likely to be made*

In short, if Caesar fails to attend the Senate today, he may lose the chance to become sole ruler of Rome; instead, he is likely to become the butt of jokes. People may even call his courage into question.

Decius apologizes; if he has been indiscreet, he says, it is his love for Caesar, and his hopes for Caesar's success, that have motivated him.

By now, Caesar's feelings have changed completely, and he is embarrassed by his earlier reluctance to leave home. He is happy to go to the Senate as originally planned, he announces.

It is at this point that Brutus, Casca and the other conspirators arrive, ready to accompany Caesar to the Senate. Caesar greets his fellow-senators warmly, and welcomes them to his home. Brutus reflects that the appearance of friendship, sadly, is not always the same as the real thing:

Caesar: Good friends, go in, and taste some wine with me;
And we, like friends, will straightway go together.
Brutus: [*Aside.*] That every like is not the same,[1] O Caesar!
The heart of Brutus earns[2] to think upon.

[1] *the fact that being like friends is not the same as being friends*
[2] *grieves, suffers*

> "Calphurnia pleads on her knee that Caesar will stay at home. Caesar at first agrees, suggesting a degree of affection and perhaps a shared apprehension between them. However, when Decius Brutus reinterprets the dream as figuring Caesar as the nurturing mother of Rome, he upstages the barren Calphurnia. By suggesting the senators will mock Caesar for placing his wife's private fears above the important public business of the State, Decius Brutus relocates fear as an exclusively womanly trait, and Caesar rejects her prescience as foolish."
>
> Alison Findlay, *Women in Shakespeare*, 2014

A warning
II, iii

News of the conspiracy has somehow leaked out. One man, Artemidorus, is determined to prevent the attack, and he has drawn up a list of the conspirators to hand to Caesar. He is waiting in a street near the Capitol, knowing that Caesar will soon pass on his way to the Senate. As he waits, he checks the contents of his note:

> *Artemidorus:* Caesar, beware of Brutus; take heed of Cassius; come not near Casca; have an eye to Cinna ... If thou beest not immortal, look about you: security gives way to conspiracy.[1] The mighty gods defend thee!
>
> [1] *freedom from suspicion allows conspiracy to succeed*

Petitions and requests are frequently handed to important senators, and Artemidorus fervently hopes that his note will attract Caesar's attention:

> *Artemidorus:* If thou read this, O Caesar, thou may'st live;
> If not, the fates with traitors do contrive.

An anxious wait
II, iv

Now that Brutus has set off on his mission, his wife Portia is at home, frantic with worry. He has told her of the planned assassination, and she is waiting anxiously by her front door.

Torn between her desire to know what is happening at the Capitol and her fear of revealing the conspiracy, she orders her servant Lucius to go to the senate-house urgently. However, in her confusion she fails to give him any instructions:

> *Portia:* I prithee, boy, run to the Senate House.
> Stay not to answer me, but get thee gone.
> Why dost thou stay?
> *Lucius:* To know my errand, madam.

Angry at her own lack of self-control, Portia forces herself to calm down, and tells Lucius that she wants to know how Brutus is; he seemed unwell when he left home this morning, she explains. She also wants Lucius to observe Caesar and his followers closely. However, while she is talking she is startled by a sudden noise, imagining it to come from the senate-house:

> *Portia:* Hark, boy, what noise is that?
> *Lucius:* I hear none, madam.
> *Portia:* Prithee, listen well.
> I heard a bustling rumour, like a fray,[1]
> And the wind brings it from the Capitol.
> *Lucius:* Sooth,[2] madam, I hear nothing.
>
> [1] *a confused, tumultuous noise, like a brawl*
> [2] *truly*

At this moment the soothsayer – who had earlier warned Caesar about the ides of March – passes by. Portia questions him insistently, wanting to know where he has come from and where he is going. When he mentions that he intends to see Caesar pass by on his way to the Capitol, Portia wants to know more. The soothsayer's replies are enigmatic:

> *Portia:* Thou hast some suit[1] to Caesar, hast thou not?
> *Soothsayer:* That I have, lady, if it will please Caesar
> To be so good to Caesar as to hear me:
> I shall beseech him to befriend himself.
> *Portia:* Why, know'st thou any harm's intended towards him?
> *Soothsayer:* None that I know will be, much that I fear may chance.
>
> [1] *request*

The soothsayer continues on his way, explaining that he needs to find a quieter spot. The streets in this area are too narrow and crowded, he says; Caesar is accompanied not only by an entourage of senators and officials, but by crowds of people who, like himself, want to attract the great man's attention.

Portia realizes that she can do nothing but wait for news from the Capitol and pray that her husband's plan is successful. Fearful that Lucius may have overheard her, she pretends to him that she is worried about a request that Brutus needs to discuss with Caesar.

Finally, exhausted by anxiety and the struggle to hide her feelings, Portia needs to be alone. She sends Lucius to the Capitol simply to pass on her best wishes to Brutus, and to assure him that she is in good spirits.

> The Globe Theatre – of which Shakespeare was a part owner – was built on marshy farmland not far from the Thames. The surrounding land tended to flood at high tide, becoming extremely muddy when the tide went out again. Despite its unpromising situation, the theatre soon became a popular venue with all classes of society.
>
> *"Recent evidence suggests that the Globe theatre opened on 12 June 1599 with Julius Caesar, after careful calculation by an astrologer to hit on the most auspicious opening day and hour. On the old calendar day that was the summer solstice, the shortest night, and it coincided with a new moon (which the almanacs judged 'best to open a new house'). A more practical consideration was that a high tide would spare the posh people in the audience from getting their clothes dirty on a long walk across smelly mudflats ... the Globe was soon a magnet for Londoners and foreign visitors."*
>
> Michael Wood, *In Search of Shakespeare*, 2003
>
> The Globe was destroyed in a fire in 1613, when Shakespeare's career was coming to an end. The theatre was rebuilt within a year, and continued successfully for almost thirty years. However, like all London theatres it was provisionally closed down in 1642, during the English Civil War. The temporary closure soon became permanent, and the theatre was demolished in 1644 to make way for housing.

The plot swings into action III, i

By now, Caesar and his companions are about to arrive at the senate-house. Caesar recognizes the soothsayer in the crowd, and points out that his earlier warning appears to have been unnecessary. The soothsayer's response, as ever, is cryptic:

> *Caesar:* The ides of March are come.
> *Soothsayer:* Ay, Caesar, but not gone.

Also in the crowd is Artemidorus, who desperately tries to hand his note to Caesar, a note that lists the conspirators who intend to carry out the assassination. Decius, anxious that nothing should disrupt their plot, intervenes, claiming that he too has a request to hand to Caesar. Artemidorus persists, but Caesar quickly loses patience with him:

> *Artemidorus:* O Caesar, read mine first; for mine's a suit
> That touches Caesar nearer. Read it, great Caesar.
> *Caesar:* What touches us ourself shall be last serv'd.
> *Artemidorus:* Delay not, Caesar. Read it instantly.
> *Caesar:* What, is the fellow mad?

Cassius, another of the conspirators, is also keen to avoid any hindrances, and he urges everyone to enter the senate-house. He is shaken when a fellow-senator wishes him well with his enterprise; has news of the conspiracy leaked out? The same senator then goes over to Caesar and starts talking to him.

Cassius and Brutus, fearing that they have been betrayed, observe the two men intently as they talk. However, their conversation seems to be an amicable one, decides Brutus; it is safe to proceed.

As planned, Trebonius has distracted Mark Antony, Caesar's right-hand man, and drawn him away from the scene. The conspirators' next step is to surround Caesar on the pretext that they have a request to make. Metellus Cimber's brother has been banished by Caesar, and Metellus himself, backed up by Brutus, Cassius, Casca and the others, is to beg for the sentence to be repealed. When Caesar is surrounded, it is Casca, they have agreed, who will strike first.

The conspirators achieve their aim

The meeting of the Senate is about to start, and Caesar calls for any petitions and complaints to be presented. Metellus, with exaggerated subservience, kneels before Caesar and begins his appeal:

Caesar: Are we all ready? What is now amiss
That Caesar and his senate must redress?
Metellus: Most high, most mighty, and most puissant[1] Caesar,
Metellus Cimber throws before thy seat[2]
An humble heart ...

[1] *powerful*
[2] *seat of judgement, throne*

The Booth family was a prominent American theatrical family of the mid-19th century. In 1864 the three Booth brothers took part in a highly acclaimed performance of *Julius Caesar* in New York. The proceeds went towards a statue of Shakespeare, still standing today, in Central Park. The youngest of the three brothers, John Wilkes Booth, played Mark Antony: however, his favourite role – and his personal hero – was Brutus.

Although from the North, Booth was fiercely pro-slavery. He despised Abraham Lincoln and regarded him as a despot: and when the opportunity presented itself, Booth, seeing himself as the upholder of liberty and destroyer of tyranny, assassinated the President in Ford's Theatre, Washington D.C., in April 1865.

Caesar interrupts immediately. He tells Metellus sternly that sycophantic behaviour might succeed with lesser men, but will not have the slightest effect on him. He is aware that Metellus is going to ask about his brother's banishment, but the law must be upheld, and the decision is irrevocable:

Caesar: Be not fond,
To think that Caesar bears such rebel blood[1]
That will be thaw'd from the true quality[2]
With that which melteth fools – I mean sweet words,
Low-crooked[3] curtsies, and base spaniel fawning.
Thy brother by decree is banished ...

[1] *don't be so foolish as to think that Caesar has such an unstable temperament*
[2] *its proper dispassionate nature*
[3] *bending, stooping*

In short, if Metellus behaves like a fawning dog, says Caesar, he must expect to be treated like one, and kicked aside without consideration. Caesar will listen to reason, but not to flattery.

Metellus, no doubt aware that Caesar would respond in this way, now turns to the other senators and asks if there are others who will speak on his behalf. Brutus comes forward and kisses Caesar's hand; he too asks for the judgement to be repealed. Cassius, falling at Caesar's feet, does the same. Caesar, becoming impatient, now lectures the senators. He explains proudly that, unlike other men, he cannot be influenced by emotional appeals, just as he does not attempt to make such appeals himself:

Caesar: I could be well mov'd, if I were as[1] you;
If I could pray to move, prayers would move me;
But I am constant as the northern star,
Of whose true-fix'd and resting quality[2]
There is no fellow in the firmament.[3]

[1] *like*
[2] *immovable, unchanging nature*
[3] *there is no equal in the heavens*

49

Just as the Northern Star is the only unchanging object amongst the countless stars in the night sky, declares Caesar, he himself is unique amongst men in his steadfast, resolute nature. His refusal to change his mind over the banishment of Metellus's brother is evidence of this firmness.

Cinna and Decius now crowd around Caesar, calling out as if they too wish to support Metellus. Caesar, exasperated, orders them away. Finally, Casca approaches. He makes no pretence of asking Caesar for any favours; the time has come to act. He draws out a dagger and plunges it into Caesar. The others immediately do the same, and Caesar is soon fatally wounded, his body covered in gashes as blows rain down on him.

Caesar is horrified when, in his dying moments, he realizes that his close friend Brutus is part of the conspiracy:

> *Cinna:* O Caesar –
> *Caesar:* Hence! Wilt thou lift up Olympus?[1]
> *Decius:* Great Caesar –
> *Caesar:* Doth not Brutus bootless[2] kneel?
> *Casca:* Speak hands[3] for me! [*They stab Caesar.*]
> *Caesar:* Et tu, Brute?[4] – Then fall Caesar! [*Dies.*]
>
> [1] *try to move a mountain*
> [2] *in vain, without effect*
> [3] *let my hands speak*
> [4] *Even you, Brutus?*

Bloody, breathless and exultant, one of the conspirators shouts out in triumph:

> *Cinna:* Liberty! Freedom! Tyranny is dead!
> Run hence, proclaim, cry it about the streets.

The aftermath

Around Caesar's bloody, lifeless body, there is chaos in the senate-house. The conspirators cry out in excitement, eager to spread the word to the people of Rome that they are free from the threat of oppression. The other senators, meanwhile, are running away in panic. Brutus tries to calm down the terrified gathering, reassuring them that there will be no more violence:

> *Brutus:* People and senators, be not affrighted.
> Fly not; stand still; ambition's debt is paid.[1]
>
> [1] *Caesar has paid in full for his ambition*

Eventually the conspirators manage to detain Publius, an elderly senator who, in his state of shock, has not managed to flee. Rejecting his companions' argument that they should prepare for retaliation from Caesar's supporters, Brutus instead talks soothingly to Publius, and asks him to spread the message to the people of Rome:

> *Metellus:* Stand fast together, lest[1] some friend of Caesar's
> Should chance –
> *Brutus:* Talk not of standing.[2] Publius, good cheer;
> There is no harm intended to your person,
> Nor to no Roman else. So tell them, Publius.
>
> [1] *in case*
> [2] *resisting, fighting*

Trebonius, who had earlier distracted Antony while the assassination took place, now returns. He reports that Antony, stunned at the news of Caesar's death, has taken refuge in his house; meanwhile, there is confusion and panic in the streets outside.

Brutus responds calmly: although they are in danger, their destinies are in the hands of fate. They must die eventually, he points out, whether now or in the distant future. In fact, Caesar's assassination has liberated him from the fear of death.

With this thought, Brutus urges all the conspirators to bathe their hands and knives in Caesar's blood. They can then march through the city and proclaim that Rome is once again free.

Cassius agrees, and as they cover their hands with Caesar's blood he predicts proudly that this event will be remembered and re-enacted by future generations:

Cassius: Stoop then, and wash. How many ages hence [1]
Shall this our lofty scene be acted over,
In states unborn, and accents [2] yet unknown!
Brutus: How many times shall Caesar bleed in sport,[3]
That now on Pompey's basis [4] lies along,
No worthier than the dust!
Cassius: So oft as that shall be,
So often shall the knot [5] of us be call'd
The men that gave their country liberty.

[1] *from now*
[2] *languages*
[3] *as entertainment, with fake blood*
[4] *at the base of Pompey's statue, where Caesar's body now lies*
[5] *group of comrades*

How many times shall Caesar bleed in sport ...

"*We in the audience, recalling what actually did result in Rome – the civil wars, the long line of despotic emperors – cannot miss the irony of their prediction, an irony that insists on our recognizing that this effort to control the consequences of an act is doomed to fail ... The leader of this assault on history, like many another reformer, is a man of high idealism, who devoutly believes that the rest of the world is like himself.*"

Maynard Mack, *Everybody's Shakespeare*, 1993

As they are about to set out into the city, a man enters the senate-house. It is Antony's servant. His message from Antony is cautious and measured: he loves and admires Brutus, just as he did Caesar, and he is prepared to hear and consider the reasons for Caesar's assassination. If Brutus gives his word that he will not be harmed, Antony is ready to talk to him.

Brutus sends the servant back to Antony, promising that his master can safely come to the senate-house. Antony will prove a good friend to the conspirators and their cause, believes Brutus. Cassius, who had originally argued for Antony to be put to death along with Caesar, is less sure:

> *Brutus:* I know that we shall have him well to friend.
> *Cassius:* I wish we may: but yet have I a mind
> That fears him much; and my misgiving still
> Falls shrewdly to the purpose.[1]
>
> [1] *my worries always turn out to be justified*

An uneasy alliance

When Antony arrives at the senate-house, he ignores Brutus's welcome. His first reaction is horror and dismay at seeing the mutilated corpse of Caesar, the great warrior and Antony's beloved friend:

> *Antony:* O mighty Caesar! dost thou lie so low?
> Are all thy conquests, glories, triumphs,[1] spoils,[2]
> Shrunk to this little measure?
>
> [1] *victory processions*
> [2] *destruction of your enemies*

If the conspirators wish to kill Antony too, he declares, this is the time and place to do it. Their hands and daggers are already covered with Caesar's blood, and Antony is perfectly willing to die alongside his friend in the senate-house.

Brutus assures Antony that, despite their bloody outward appearance, he and the other assassins have acted purely out of compassion for Rome and its people, which must outweigh their love for Caesar. They bear no ill will towards Antony, and still regard him as a friend and brother. Cassius adds that they hope Antony will play a part in sharing out the titles and responsibilities that were previously Caesar's.

Brutus promises Antony that they will soon tell him, in detail, why Caesar's death was necessary. However, the most urgent task at the moment is to go out into the city and pacify the agitated, fearful crowds in the streets of Rome.

Antony appears to accept Brutus's assurance, and even goes as far as to shake hands with each one of the conspirators. Surrounded by Caesar's killers, he realizes that he is in a difficult, even dangerous situation as a friend and supporter of Caesar. It will seem to others either that he is afraid to avenge his friend's death, or that he is trying to win the assassins' favour:

> *Antony:* ... alas, what shall I say?
> My credit[1] now stands on such slippery ground,
> That one of two bad ways you must conceit[2] me,
> Either a coward, or a flatterer.
>
> [1] *reputation, credibility*
> [2] *imagine, consider*

Antony then addresses Caesar's corpse once more, asking his forgiveness for making peace with his killers. He should instead be weeping profusely, just as Caesar is bleeding:

> *Antony:* Had I as many eyes as thou hast wounds,
> Weeping as fast as they stream forth thy blood,
> It would become me better than to close
> In terms of friendship with thine enemies.

Antony's lament over Caesar's body is eventually interrupted by Cassius. Antony's praise for Caesar is understandable, he says, but Cassius, Brutus and the others need to know the truth: can they count on Antony as a friend and ally? Antony assures them that they can, on the condition that he is given complete and conclusive reasons for Caesar's assassination.

Brutus promises Antony that reasons will be produced that fully justify the conspirators' actions. Antony says that this is enough to satisfy him, but he has one request: that he can address the people of Rome, as Caesar's friend, at the funeral. Brutus agrees to his request.

At this point Cassius takes Brutus aside and tells him, furiously, that he is making a mistake. Antony is likely to arouse dangerous emotions amongst the crowd:

> *Cassius:* Brutus, a word with you.
> [*Aside.*] You know not what you do. Do not consent
> That Antony speak in his funeral.
> Know you how much the people may be mov'd
> By that which he will utter?

Brutus rejects his argument. He himself will speak first, he explains, and justify Caesar's death to the crowd. He will make it clear that Antony, following him, speaks with Brutus's full permission. The fact that Caesar will have a proper burial, with a funeral oration spoken by his closest friend, will show the conspirators in a good light, says Brutus: but Cassius remains deeply apprehensive.

Brutus now turns to Antony once more. Antony may take Caesar's body to the market-place, where the funeral will be held, and address the crowd. However, as Brutus has just discussed with Cassius, he must observe certain conditions:

Brutus: You shall not in your funeral speech blame us,
But speak all good you can devise of Caesar,
And say you do't by our permission;
Else shall you not have any hand at all
About his funeral. And you shall speak
In the same pulpit whereto I am going,
After my speech is ended.

Antony is satisfied. As the others leave the senate-house, he stays behind to prepare Caesar's body.

> "I cannot help feeling that the majority of past critics have been misled by Brutus's estimate of himself into regarding him as a more wholly admirable person than Shakespeare intended him to be ... Shakespeare's Brutus is, with all his estimable qualities, pompous, opinionated and self-righteous. His judgement is not to be trusted ... At almost every crisis in his fortunes he makes decisions, against the advice of experienced men of the world, that contribute materially to the failure of his cause. He seems completely blind to reality, an ineffectual idealist whose idealism cannot prevent him from committing a senseless and terrible crime."
>
> T. S. Dorsch, Introduction to the Arden edition of *Julius Caesar*, 1955

Antony plans to strike back

Alone with Caesar's corpse, Antony now reveals his true feelings:

> *Antony:* O, pardon me, thou bleeding piece of earth,
> That I am meek and gentle with these butchers.
> Thou art the ruins of the noblest man
> That ever lived in the tide of times.[1]
> Woe to the hand that shed this costly[2] blood!
>
> [1] *in the ever-changing course of history*
> [2] *precious*

Antony foresees violent civil war as the perpetrators of this murder are hunted down and killed. Wherever the culprits try to hide, the ghost of Caesar will track them down and inflict terrible vengeance on them:

> *Antony:* ... Caesar's spirit, ranging for revenge,
> With Ate[1] by his side come hot from hell,
> Shall in these confines[2] with a monarch's voice
> Cry 'Havoc!'[3] and let slip[4] the dogs of war ...
>
> [1] *the goddess of retribution and destruction*
> [2] *these regions, throughout Rome*
> [3] *a battle cry meaning 'no mercy'; the signal for unrestricted slaughter and looting*
> [4] *unleash*

A man now enters the senate-house, and Antony recognizes him as the servant of the young Octavius, Caesar's great-nephew and adopted heir. Caesar recently contacted Octavius and asked him to come to Rome: his servant has come to confirm that he is on his way.

Just as the man is delivering the news, he sees the bloodstained corpse on the senate-house floor. Realising it is Caesar, he is overcome with shock and sorrow. Antony, on the verge of weeping himself, gives the servant time to shed his tears:

> *Antony:* ... get thee apart and weep.
> Passion, I see, is catching, for mine eyes,
> Seeing those beads of sorrow stand in thine,
> Begin to water.

The man eventually continues with his message, and tells Antony that Octavius is not far from Rome.

Antony's first thought is that the servant must hurry back to tell Octavius the news of Caesar's death, and warn him to stay away from the city, which is now in a dangerous, chaotic state. However, on reflection he decides that the servant should remain for the funeral. It is not yet clear how the people of Rome will respond to Caesar's assassination, and Antony intends, in his funeral speech, to assess their reaction. When that is known, the servant is to report back to Octavius.

Finally, Antony asks for the man's help, and the two of them carry Caesar's body out of the empty senate-house: it is to be taken to the market-place, where it will be displayed to the people of Rome.

Brutus persuades the crowd III, ii

In the Roman forum, the busy market-place in the city centre, the atmosphere is tense and angry. Julius Caesar was a military hero and a popular figure, and the people of Rome are demanding an explanation for his death.

Brutus and Cassius have come to address the crowd. The gathering is so large that Brutus decides to send Cassius to speak in a different part of the city, taking part of the crowd with him.

Brutus himself goes up into the public pulpit. Asking his audience to listen patiently, he emphasizes, using formal rhetoric, that he is an honourable man with a good cause:

> *Brutus:* Romans, countrymen, and lovers,[1] hear me for my cause, and be silent, that[2] you may hear. Believe me for mine honour, and have respect to mine honour,[3] that you may believe.
>
> [1] *beloved friends*
> [2] *so that*
> [3] *bear in mind the fact that I am honourable*

Brutus goes on to say how much he loved and admired Caesar. However, he tells his listeners, despite his greatness, Caesar had one fatal flaw: he was ambitious. And if his ambition had been achieved, the free citizens of the Roman Republic would have been reduced to virtual slaves, under the rule of one all-powerful individual. Despite Caesar's personal qualities and his military victories, his death was necessary for the well-being of Rome:

> *Brutus:* Had you rather Caesar were living, and die all slaves, than that Caesar were dead, to live all free men? As Caesar loved me, I weep for him; as he was fortunate, I rejoice at it; as he was valiant, I honour him; but, as he was ambitious, I slew him.

He asks the crowd directly whether any of them are happy to lose their freedom, or do not care about the state of Rome, or do not love their country; if so, he apologizes, for his speech may have offended them. At this point he pauses for a response; and the crowd shouts out in approval.

Brutus now announces that details of Caesar's life, and his death, have been entered in the historical records, in the Capitol. In those records, full credit has been given for his achievements; and his faults, for which he has paid the ultimate price, have not been exaggerated.

Mark Antony now arrives, carrying Caesar's body. Brutus draws the crowd's attention to Antony: although he played no part in Caesar's death, says Brutus, he will benefit, as they all will, by living in freedom and equality:

> *Brutus:* Here comes his body, mourned by Mark Antony, who, though he had no hand in his death, shall receive the benefit of his dying, a place in the commonwealth, as which of you shall not?

If Brutus ever falls short of the ideals of the Roman Republic, he is prepared to die by the same dagger that killed his dear friend Caesar. The crowd again roars in support of Brutus, calling for him to be carried triumphantly through the streets as their leader:

> *1st Plebeian:* Bring him with triumph home unto his house.
> *2nd Plebeian:* Give him a statue with his ancestors.[1]
> *3rd Plebeian:* Let him be Caesar.
> *4th Plebeian:* Caesar's better parts[2]
> Shall be crown'd in Brutus.
>
> [1] *Brutus's ancestors included Lucius Junius Brutus, founder of the Republic*
> [2] *qualities*

Brutus now tells the crowd that he must leave them: however, he insists that, rather than accompanying him in procession, they must remain in the forum to hear Antony's speech. Antony was a renowned supporter of Caesar, and Brutus has agreed that he may pay tribute to him:

> *Brutus:* ... for my sake, stay here with Antony.
> Do grace[1] to Caesar's corpse, and grace his speech
> Tending to Caesar's glories,[2] which Mark Antony,
> By our permission, is allow'd to make.
>
> [1] *pay respect*
> [2] *give a respectful hearing to Antony's speech, which will relate to Caesar's glories*

Brutus leaves, and Antony takes his place in the pulpit.

Antony remembers his friend

The general opinion in the crowd is that Brutus was right, and they are fortunate to be rid of Caesar. However, although the plebeians' earlier anger has subsided, there is still a great deal of noisy discussion among the crowd, and Antony struggles to make himself heard.

Eventually, Antony has the crowd's attention. Although Brutus has allowed him to speak of his admiration for his dead friend, says Antony, he does not intend to do so. People's good qualities are often forgotten after their death, and inevitably the same will happen with Caesar:

> *Antony:* Friends, Romans, countrymen, lend me your ears;
> I come to bury Caesar, not to praise him.
> The evil that men do lives after them,
> The good is oft interred[1] with their bones;
> So let it be with Caesar.
>
> [1] *buried*

Besides, whatever Caesar's good qualities may have been, Brutus has already explained that he was ambitious for power. If true, this was indeed a terrible flaw in his character, says Antony. His own experience of Caesar was very different, but Brutus, as an honourable man, must be telling the truth:

> *Antony:*   The noble Brutus
> Hath told you Caesar was ambitious.
> If it were so, it was a grievous fault,
> And grievously hath Caesar answer'd it.
> Here, under leave[1] of Brutus and the rest,
> (For Brutus is an honourable man,
> So are they all, all honourable men)
> Come I to speak in Caesar's funeral.
> He was my friend, faithful and just to me;
> But Brutus says he was ambitious,
> And Brutus is an honourable man.
>
> [1] *by permission*

Antony goes on to examine the nature of the ambition attributed to Caesar. Failing to find any examples, he can only repeat that the word of the honourable Brutus must be accepted:

> *Antony:* He hath brought many captives home to Rome,
> Whose ransoms did the general coffers fill: [1]
> Did this in Caesar seem ambitious?
> When that the poor have cried, Caesar hath wept;
> Ambition should be made of sterner stuff:
> Yet Brutus says he was ambitious,
> And Brutus is an honourable man.
> You all did see that on the Lupercal
> I thrice presented him a kingly crown,
> Which he did thrice refuse. Was this ambition?
> Yet Brutus says he was ambitious,
> And sure he is an honourable man.

[1] *filled the public treasury*

Antony is simply speaking from his own experience, he claims, and is not attempting to refute Brutus's version of the truth. At this point, he seems to be overcome with emotion, and suddenly asks the crowd why they too are not dismayed at Caesar's death:

> *Antony:* You all did love him once, not without cause;
> What cause withholds you then to mourn for him?
> O judgement, thou art fled to brutish beasts,
> And men have lost their reason.

He apologizes for his outburst: reminding his listeners of the coffin nearby, he explains that his heart is still with Caesar. He needs time to regain his composure, he claims, and pauses for a few minutes.

By now, the mood of the crowd has changed considerably. The people have become quieter and more thoughtful. Perhaps Caesar was not the tyrant that Brutus had portrayed; in fact, his refusal to accept the crown when it was offered at the Lupercalian festival suggests the opposite.

Antony's emotional turmoil has moved his audience, too. The general feeling is that he is an honest, noble man; and when he returns to the pulpit they listen attentively.

A distressing sight

Resuming his speech, Antony hints that the people of Rome would be furious if they knew the goodwill that Caesar had felt towards them. It would be wrong to disclose any more, he says, because he does not wish to contradict the impression given by the honourable Brutus and Cassius. However, he is prepared to reveal that he knows the contents of Caesar's will: and at this moment he produces the document itself.

There is uproar in the crowd as all those present cry out, unanimously, for Antony to read the will. He insists that he cannot, while revealing that the beneficiaries of the will include the people of Rome themselves:

Antony: Have patience, gentle friends; I must not read it.
It is not meet[1] you know how Caesar lov'd you.
You are not wood, you are not stones, but men;
And being men, hearing the will of Caesar,
It will inflame you, it will make you mad.
'Tis good you know not that you are his heirs ...

[1] *right, appropriate*

At this news, the commotion grows even more strident. When Antony once again mentions the conspirators, the response is angry jeering:

Antony: Will you be patient? Will you stay awhile?
I have o'ershot myself[1] to tell you of it.
I fear I wrong the honourable men
Whose daggers have stabb'd Caesar; I do fear it.
4th Plebeian: They were traitors. Honourable men!
All: The will! – The testament!
2nd Plebeian: They were villains, murderers! The will! Read the will!

[1] *gone further than I intended; said too much*

63

Antony finally agrees to read the will; but first, he wishes to show everyone Caesar's body. He asks the people's permission to do so, and the crowd willingly makes way for Antony as he comes down from the pulpit and walks over to the bier on which the corpse is lying.

As the people start to gather round the body, Antony warns them that it will be a distressing sight. He starts by contemplating Caesar's torn, bloodstained clothing, and reminds the crowd of a famous military victory against a powerful enemy tribe:

> *Antony:* If you have tears, prepare to shed them now.
> You all do know this mantle.[1] I remember
> The first time ever Caesar put it on;
> 'Twas on a summer's evening in his tent,
> That day he overcame the Nervii.
>
> [1] *cloak*

Looking more closely at the cloak, he points out, one by one, the wounds inflicted by the conspirators. The final and most cruel of these was the work of Brutus, Caesar's much-loved friend:

> *Antony:* Look, in this place ran Cassius' dagger through:
> See what a rent[1] the envious[2] Casca made:
> Through this the well-beloved Brutus stabb'd;
> ... This was the most unkindest cut of all;
> For when the noble Caesar saw him stab,
> Ingratitude, more strong than traitors' arms,
> Quite vanquish'd[3] him: then burst his mighty heart ...
>
> [1] *gash, tear*
> [2] *malicious*
> [3] *utterly defeated*

Soon the onlookers are in tears. Antony praises them for their compassion; but they have only seen Caesar's cloak. The sight of the body itself is even more painful, he warns.

At this moment he pulls away the cloak to reveal the gashed, mutilated corpse, and the passions in the crowd reach new heights:

> *1st Plebeian:* O piteous spectacle!
> *2nd Plebeian:* O noble Caesar!
> *3rd Plebeian:* O woeful day!
> *4th Plebeian:* O traitors! Villains!
> *1st Plebeian:* O most bloody sight!
> *2nd Plebeian:* We will be revenged.

Caesar's will is made public

The call for revenge sweeps through the crowd, and they are eager to seek out and kill the conspirators. However, Antony asks them to wait. He now has complete control of the crowd, and they listen attentively. His is not trying to provoke them to violent action, he claims. Caesar's killers no doubt had good reasons; all Antony is doing is mourning his friend.

> *Antony:* … They that have done this deed are honourable.
> What private griefs they have, alas, I know not,
> That made them do it. They are wise and honourable,
> And will, no doubt, with reasons answer you.
> I come not, friends, to steal away your hearts.
> I am no orator, as Brutus is,
> But (as you know me all) a plain blunt man …

If he had the eloquence of Brutus, suggests Antony, he could rouse the whole city to mutiny. At the mention of the word, the people immediately respond by calling for mutiny, and again they resolve to set out and kill the traitors.

Antony manages to hold back the crowd with one final announcement. He reminds them that they have not yet heard the contents of Caesar's will. He opens it now and reveals that Caesar has left every citizen the equivalent of more than two months' wages:

> *Antony:* To every Roman citizen he gives,
> To every several[1] man, seventy-five drachmas.
> *2nd Plebeian:* Most noble Caesar! We'll revenge his death.
>
> [1] *individual*

In addition, Caesar has bequeathed many of his private parks and gardens to the people of Rome in perpetuity. Caesar was a great man, declares Antony. The angry citizens now set off to cremate Caesar's body with the reverence it deserves; after that, they will burn down the conspirators' houses.

Antony makes no further attempt to hold them back. He is confident that disorder and rioting in the streets of Rome will help to bring about the destruction of his enemies:

> *Antony:* Here was a Caesar! When comes such another?
> *1st Plebeian:* Never, never! Come, away, away!
> We'll burn his body in the holy place,
> And with the brands[1] fire the traitors' houses.
> Take up the body.
> *2nd Plebeian:* Go fetch fire.
> *3rd Plebeian:* Pluck down benches.
> *4th Plebeian:* Pluck down forms, windows,[2] any thing.
> *Antony:* Now let it work.[3] Mischief, thou art afoot,
> Take thou what course thou wilt!
>
> [1] *burning pieces of wood*
> [2] *long benches and wooden shutters*
> [3] *let events take their own course*

The servant of young Octavius, Caesar's heir, now arrives. His master has come to Rome, he announces, and is in Caesar's house with Lepidus who, like Antony, was a close ally of Caesar's. Antony is pleased: there is a power vacuum in Rome, and the three of them urgently need to discuss their next steps.

The servant mentions that Brutus and Cassius have been seen riding frantically out of the city: no doubt they have heard that the people of Rome have turned violently against them.

> In Shakespeare's time, play scripts were the property of the theatre company for which they were written. They were a valuable asset, and companies were generally unwilling to publish them, particularly while a play was still popular and attracting audiences. At least half of Shakespeare's plays, for example, were not published during his lifetime.
>
> In time, however, plays gradually came to be regarded, like poetry, as valid works of literature. Five years after Shakespeare's death, John Heminges and Henry Condell, two of his fellow-actors, set about the task of creating a complete edition of Shakespeare's plays, including introductory material and an engraving of the author. The resulting book, now known as the 'First Folio', was published in 1623. This collected edition contained many plays – including *The Tempest*, *Macbeth*, and *Julius Caesar* – which would otherwise have been lost for ever.

An innocent victim III, iii

A poet named Cinna is wandering through the streets of Rome. Last night he dreamed about Caesar, and now, on his way to the funeral, he is weighed down with a sense of anxiety.

Suddenly Cinna is confronted by an unruly mob of citizens. They fire questions at him aggressively:

> *1st Plebeian:* What is your name?
> *2nd Plebeian:* Whither [1] are you going?
> *3rd Plebeian:* Where do you dwell?
> *4th Plebeian:* Are you a married man or a bachelor?
> *2nd Plebeian:* Answer every man directly.
> *1st Plebeian:* Ay, and briefly.
> *4th Plebeian:* Ay, and wisely.
> *3rd Plebeian:* Ay, and truly, you were best.[2]

> [1] *where*
> [2] *it would be best; if you know what's good for you*

When they learn that the man's name is Cinna, they assault him violently, believing him to be one of the conspirators. He pleads with them, explaining that he is not the Cinna who took part in the assassination, but by now his attackers are out for blood, and refuse to listen to reason:

> *3rd Plebeian:* Your name, sir, truly.
> *Cinna:* Truly, my name is Cinna.
> *1st Plebeian:* Tear him to pieces! He's a conspirator.
> *Cinna:* I am Cinna the poet, I am Cinna the poet.
> *4th Plebeian:* Tear him for his bad verses, tear him for his bad verses.
> *Cinna:* I am not Cinna the conspirator.
> *1st Plebeian:* It is no matter, his name's Cinna ...

The citizens, shouting ferociously, are bent on continuing their violent spree. Dragging Cinna's battered body with them, they set out for the conspirators' houses, determined to burn them to the ground.

The 1590s were a dangerous time for English dramatists. The response of the authorities to perceived criticism could be unpredictable and aggressive. Although Shakespeare himself had managed to keep out of trouble, several of his contemporaries had suffered in various ways:

"Shakespeare had seen the innocent Thomas Kyd broken by torture on the rack, Christopher Marlowe possibly assassinated, and Ben Jonson imprisoned ... In a grim replay of the scene in which Caesar is hacked to death in the Capitol, an innocent poet is savagely murdered onstage. It's hard not to conclude that the haze of Elizabethan censorship hanging in the air at this time seeps into the play at such moments ..."

James Shapiro, *1599: A Year in the Life of William Shakespeare*, 2005

The counter-attack is prepared IV, i

In the chaos that Caesar's assassination has left in its wake, three men – Antony, Octavius and Lepidus – are planning to take control of the Republic. They have met to draw up a list of their enemies; anyone who might stand in their way is to be eliminated. Caesar's killers and their associates are included on the list, but they are not the only ones:

Antony: These many then shall die; their names are prick'd.[1]
Octavius: Your brother too must die; consent you, Lepidus?
Lepidus: I do consent –
Octavius: Prick him down, Antony.
Lepidus: Upon condition Publius shall not live,
Who is your sister's son, Mark Antony.
Antony: He shall not live. Look, with a spot I damn him.[2]

[1] *marked*
[2] *condemn him to death*

These many then shall die ...

Caesar's assassination was followed, as Shakespeare describes, by a wave of killings – known as the 'proscriptions' – ordered by the three men who planned to seize power. The stated aim of the aspiring leaders was to avenge the death of Caesar, and to prevent outright anarchy and civil war. They also took the opportunity to remove potential enemies and confiscate their property.

Substantial rewards were offered for the killing of proscribed individuals. Those suspected of sheltering anyone on the list – or failing to come forward with information – could also be put to death. Thousands of people died in the violence that ensued.

Antony asks Lepidus to go to Caesar's house and fetch the will. It may be possible, he believes, to reduce the amount paid out in legacies so that the three of them will have more funds for their own purposes.

When Lepidus has left, Antony makes it clear to Octavius that he has a low opinion of their ally:

> *Antony:* This is a slight unmeritable man,
> Meet[1] to be sent on errands. Is it fit,
> The three-fold world[2] divided, he should stand
> One of the three to share it?
>
> [1] *suitable*
> [2] *the Roman world of Europe, Asia and north Africa*

Octavius remarks that Antony seemed content to include him in their power-sharing negotiations. Antony replies, cynically, that Lepidus will provide useful cover against the criticism that will inevitably come their way. Once the two of them have gained control of the Republic, Lepidus can be cast aside like an unwanted beast of burden:

> *Antony:* … though we lay these honours[1] on this man,
> To ease ourselves of divers sland'rous loads,[2]
> He shall but bear them as the ass bears gold …
>   … having brought our treasure where we will,
> Then take we down his load, and turn him off,[3]
> Like to the empty[4] ass, to shake his ears,
> And graze in commons.[5]
>
> [1] *official titles, powers*
> [2] *to lighten the weight of the blame which will be laid upon us*
> [3] *send him away*
> [4] *unburdened*
> [5] *on public pasture-land*

Octavius argues that Lepidus is an experienced, courageous soldier. Antony does not disagree; however, his horse has courage, too, he tells the young man, but that does not mean that it is the equal of its master.

In short, Lepidus may be a useful, manageable subordinate, but he lacks the dynamism and imagination of a true leader:

> *Antony:* ... He must be taught, and train'd, and bid go forth:
> A barren-spirited[1] fellow; one that feeds
> On objects, arts, and imitations,[2]
> Which, out of use and stal'd by other men,
> Begin his fashion.[3]
>
> [1] *lacking initiative or originality*
> [2] *a person who is interested in curiosities, and second-hand ideas and fashions*
> [3] *which, though other people have grown tired of them, are his starting-point*

Antony now comes on to a more pressing topic. Brutus and Cassius have raised an army, and he and Octavius must respond in the same way, and combine their forces. At the same time, they need to be sure of their supporters, and root out any opposition within their own ranks:

> *Antony:* ... let our alliance be combin'd,
> Our best friends made, our means stretch'd;[1]
> And let us presently go sit in council,
> How covert matters may be best disclos'd,
> And open perils surest answered.[2]
>
> [1] *let us establish who our strongest supporters are, and extend our resources as far as possible*
> [2] *to discuss how hidden threats may be brought to light, and clear dangers most securely dealt with*

Octavius agrees. There are potential rivals and conspirators all around them:

Octavius: Let us do so: for we are at the stake,[1]
And bay'd about [2] with many enemies;
And some that smile have in their hearts, I fear,
Millions of mischiefs.

[1] *tied to the stake, like bears in a bear-baiting arena*
[2] *surrounded by fierce, barking dogs*

> *... we are at the stake,*
> *And bay'd about with many enemies ...*
>
> A few minutes' walk from the Globe Theatre, where *Julius Caesar* was first performed, was the Bear Garden, a large open-air arena. A German traveller of the time describes a visit:
>
> *"Without the city are some theatres, where English actors represent almost every day comedies and tragedies to very numerous audiences ... There is still another place, built in the form of a theatre, which serves for the baiting of bears and bulls. They are fastened behind, and then worried by those great English dogs and mastiffs ... To this entertainment there often follows that of whipping a blinded bear, which is performed by five or six men, standing in a circle with whips, which they exercise upon him without any mercy. He cannot escape from them because of his chains ..."*
>
> Paul Hentzner, *Travels in England*, 1598

An uncomfortable meeting IV, ii

Months have passed since the death of Caesar, and Brutus and Cassius, having fled Rome, have travelled hundreds of miles to the east. They have both raised armies in Rome's eastern provinces, and the two men have arranged to join forces near the city of Sardis, in Asia Minor.

Brutus is now camped, with his army, near Sardis. Cassius is approaching, and has sent his servant Pindarus ahead to greet Brutus. It immediately becomes clear that Brutus is displeased with his ally:

> *Brutus:* Your master, Pindarus,
> In his own change, or by ill officers,[1]
> Hath given me some worthy cause to wish
> Things done undone ...
>
> [1] *because he has changed in some way, or through the actions of bad subordinates*

Brutus and Pindarus agree, diplomatically, that the differences between the two leaders can easily be settled. However, Brutus then takes his lieutenant Lucilius to one side. Lucilius has just visited Cassius, and Brutus wants to know how Cassius behaved towards him.

The lieutenant's answer is not encouraging, and Brutus suspects that his fellow-conspirator may be losing his enthusiasm for their partnership:

> *Brutus:* A word, Lucilius;
> How he receiv'd you, let me be resolv'd.[1]
> *Lucilius:* With courtesy and with respect enough,
> But not with such familiar instances,[2]
> Nor with such free and friendly conference,[3]
> As he hath us'd of old.

Brutus: Thou hast describ'd
A hot friend cooling. Ever note, Lucilius,
When love begins to sicken and decay
It useth an enforced ceremony.[4]

[1] *describe to me how Cassius treated you*
[2] *signs of friendship and familiarity*
[3] *conversation*
[4] *strained formality*

If Cassius' goodwill towards Brutus is starting to cool, this does not bode well for their alliance; when put to the test, believes Brutus, his loyalty may fail.

At this point, Cassius enters, leading his army. Like Brutus, he feels that their friendship is at risk, and he wastes no time in expressing his resentment. Brutus's lofty answer does nothing to calm him down:

Cassius: Most noble brother, you have done me wrong.
Brutus: Judge me, you gods; wrong I mine enemies?
And if not so, how should I wrong a brother?
Cassius: Brutus, this sober form[1] of yours hides wrongs ...

[1] *dignified outward appearance*

Brutus immediately silences Cassius: they must not be seen to be arguing in public, he insists. Both men give orders for their troops to be moved out of earshot, and they go into Brutus's tent to continue their discussion.

Brutus and Cassius fall out IV, iii

Alone with Brutus, Cassius at once launches into an account of his grievance. One of his followers, accused of taking bribes, has been publicly disgraced by Brutus. Cassius' letters pleading on the man's behalf have been completely disregarded.

Brutus answers that Cassius should not have written in the man's defence. Cassius declares angrily that this is no time to quibble over offences such as that supposedly committed by his follower.

The argument intensifies as Brutus accuses Cassius himself of having a reputation for being corrupt:

> Brutus: Let me tell you, Cassius, you yourself
> Are much condemn'd to have an itching palm,[1]
> To sell and mart your offices[2] for gold
> To undeservers.
>
> [1] *widely accused of having a mercenary streak*
> [2] *trade important official positions*

At this, Cassius can barely restrain his fury: any other man would die for talking to him like this. He is almost speechless with rage when Brutus calmly tells him that it is only his honourable name that has saved him from punishment. Brutus then goes on to recall the noble ideals of freedom and justice that originally inspired them, ideals that Cassius is in danger of betraying:

> Brutus: Remember March, the ides of March remember.
> Did not great Julius bleed for justice' sake?
> What villain touch'd his body, that did stab,
> And not for justice?
> ... shall we now
> Contaminate our fingers with base bribes,
> And sell the mighty space of our large honours[1]
> For so much trash as may be grasped thus?[2]
> I had rather be a dog, and bay[3] the moon,
> Than such a Roman.
>
> [1] *our vast capacity for honour and magnanimity*
> [2] *as much money as we can get our hands on*
> [3] *howl at*

Cassius argues that, with his long experience as a soldier, he knows better than Brutus how to deal with people. If Brutus provokes him any further, he warns, he is likely to lose his temper completely and become violent. Nevertheless, Brutus continues to defy him, telling him that becoming angry and making threats should be beneath him:

> Brutus: Hear me, for I will speak.
> Must I give way and room to your rash choler?[1]

	Shall I be frighted when a madman stares?
Cassius:	O ye gods, ye gods! Must I endure all this?
Brutus:	All this? Ay, more: fret till your proud heart break; Go show your slaves how choleric you are … … By the gods, You shall digest the venom of your spleen,[2] Though[3] it do split you …

[1] *let your irrational anger have free rein*
[2] *swallow the poison of your fiery temper*
[3] *even if*

Brutus is indifferent to Cassius' threats, he claims, and even amused by them; his own honesty is his protection. As the quarrel continues, Brutus reveals a deeper reason for his displeasure. Needing money to fund his army, and refusing to stoop to the level of extorting money from the local population, he had earlier contacted Cassius to ask for financial help. When Cassius refused, Brutus was deeply wounded by his friend's pettiness and meanness.

If the tables had been turned, maintains Brutus, he would not have hesitated to help his friend. They are fighting in a noble cause, and financial considerations are trivial in comparison. Cassius claims that there has been a misunderstanding: he did not refuse to help Brutus. The fault lay with the messenger, who failed to pass on Cassius' message correctly:

Brutus:	I did send To you for gold to pay my legions, Which you denied me: was that done like Cassius? Should I have answer'd Caius Cassius so? When Marcus Brutus grows so covetous, To lock such rascal counters[1] from his friends, Be ready, gods, with all your thunderbolts, Dash him to pieces!
Cassius:	I denied you not.
Brutus:	You did.
Cassius:	I did not. He was but a fool That brought my answer back.

[1] *worthless tokens; coins*

Reconciliation

Cassius, almost overcome with emotion, accuses Brutus of rejecting their friendship. Brutus insists that he is only telling the truth, and refusing to flatter him:

Cassius: Brutus hath riv'd[1] my heart.
A friend should bear his friend's infirmities;
But Brutus makes mine greater than they are.
Brutus: I do not, till you practise them on me.
Cassius: You love me not.
Brutus: I do not like your faults.
Cassius: A friendly eye could never see such faults.
Brutus: A flatterer's would not, though they do appear
As huge as high Olympus.

[1] *split, broken*

Dispirited and exhausted, Cassius now makes a dramatic gesture, taking out a knife and inviting Brutus to kill him. Brutus pacifies him, promising that he will always tolerate his friend's rages and insults:

Cassius: There is my dagger,
And here my naked breast ...
I, that denied thee gold, will give my heart:
Strike, as thou didst at Caesar; for I know,
When thou didst hate him worst, thou lov'dst him better
Than ever thou lov'dst Cassius.
Brutus: Sheathe your dagger.
Be angry when you will, it shall have scope;[1]
Do what you will, dishonour shall be humour.[2]

[1] *your anger will be given free play; I will not stop you from expressing your anger*
[2] *I will take any dishonourable insults as excusable quirks of your temperament*

By now, Brutus has calmed down. He himself, unlike Cassius, rarely gives way to anger, he says; and when he does, he quickly regains his composure. Cassius, however, is still unhappy. In particular, he is resentful that Brutus had earlier claimed to be amused by Cassius' angry threats. Brutus replies that he too had been speaking in anger:

Cassius: Hath Cassius liv'd
To be but mirth and laughter to his Brutus,
When grief and blood ill-temper'd vexeth him?[1]
Brutus: When I spoke that, I was ill-temper'd too.
Cassius: Do you confess so much? Give me your hand.
Brutus: And my heart too.

[1] *when Cassius is tormented by painful emotions arising from his volatile temperament*

Cassius eagerly seizes on his friend's apology, and the two men embrace. His anger fading, Cassius tells Brutus that he inherited his fiery temperament from his mother. Brutus teases him: he will forgive Cassius' angry outbursts in future, imagining that it his mother's voice, not that of Cassius, that he is hearing.

In New York in 1937, Orson Welles' adaptation of *Julius Caesar*, subtitled *Death of a Dictator*, was widely regarded as the theatrical sensation of the year. The stark, severely lit stage was reminiscent of the Nuremberg Rallies, the Nazi Party's annual propaganda events of the time; Caesar bore a strong resemblance to Mussolini; and most of the senators wore black military uniforms and jackboots.

The 22-year-old Welles seemed to be exploring, through the play, how to respond to the dictatorships that were on the rise in Germany, Italy and Spain. He played Brutus himself, regarding him as the play's central character rather than Caesar. However, his view of the role was far from heroic:

"Brutus is the classical picture of the eternal, impotent, ineffectual, fumbling liberal; the reformer who wants to do something about things but doesn't know how ... he's the bourgeois intellectual who, under a modern dictatorship, would be the first to be put up against a wall and shot."

Orson Welles, *The Mercury*, 1937

A tragic event comes to light

There is a sudden commotion as a man forces his way past the guards and into Brutus's tent. The man has, presumably, overheard the earlier argument between the two men, and is determined to bring the dispute to an end.

It emerges that the man is a poet. Whilst Cassius is amused, Brutus is furious at the interruption. They need to plan their campaign against Octavius and Antony, and a poet's thoughts are irrelevant:

Poet: Love, and be friends, as two such men should be;
For I have seen more years,[1] I'm sure, than ye.
Cassius: Ha, ha! How vildly[2] doth this cynic[3] rhyme!
Brutus: Get you hence, sirrah! Saucy fellow, hence!
Cassius: Bear with him, Brutus; 'tis his fashion.
Brutus: I'll know his humour, when he knows his time.[4]
What should the wars do with these jigging[5] fools?

[1] *I am older and more experienced*
[2] *vilely*
[3] *blunt-speaking critic (of our behaviour)*
[4] *I'll tolerate his eccentricity when he understands that there's a proper time for it*
[5] *rhyming, versifying*

The intrusion of the poet into Brutus's tent is usually cut from modern productions. It is difficult for us to make sense of this bizarre episode in which a poet barges into the tent, speaks a few lines of bad verse (in a misguided attempt to reconcile two men who have just been reconciled) and is bundled out again.

The significance of the incident – if any – is lost on us. Is it a comment on the disputes, rife at the time, between rival poets? A final brief appearance for William Kempe, the comic actor who was about to leave the company? A reference to censorship? A parody of the sermon that theatregoers may have heard earlier in the day? Or a self-mocking statement of the irrelevance of poetry? We can only guess.

Eventually the poet is ejected from the tent. Brutus, still angry, calls for some wine. Cassius, now in good humour, is surprised at his friend's reaction to the intrusion, particularly as Brutus is a renowned follower of the philosophy of Stoicism. It emerges that a tragic event lies behind Brutus's erratic mood:

Cassius: I did not think you could have been so angry.
Brutus: O Cassius, I am sick of many griefs.
Cassius: Of your philosophy you make no use,
If you give place to accidental evils.[1]
Brutus: No man bears sorrow better. Portia is dead.

[1] *if you are upset by unfortunate events that happen by chance*

Cassius is stunned. He is horrified that he has just been arguing bitterly with Brutus without realizing that his beloved wife Portia had recently died. He asks how she died, and Brutus reveals that she committed suicide in an agonizing manner:

Brutus: Impatient of[1] my absence,
And grief that young Octavius with Mark Antony
Have made themselves so strong[2] …
… With this she fell distract,[3]
And, her attendants absent, swallow'd fire.[4]
Cassius: And died so?
Brutus: Even so.
Cassius: O ye immortal gods!

[1] *distressed by*
[2] *have combined their forces, to oppose Brutus*
[3] *distraught, frantic*
[4] *choked herself with red-hot coals*

Portia's death must not be mentioned again, says Brutus. At this point a servant arrives, bringing some candles; it has grown dark while Brutus and Cassius have been talking. The servant brings wine, too, and in the candlelight the two friends drink deeply.

81

A disagreement over strategy

Messala, a Roman nobleman who supports the Republican cause of Brutus and Cassius, now arrives. He confirms the news that Brutus has already heard: that Octavius and Mark Antony have brought together a mighty army, and are advancing eastwards towards them. Their next destination is Philippi, in northern Greece.

Messala mentions that the proscriptions – the murders of suspected opponents, decreed by the three aspiring leaders of Rome – have been even more ruthless than expected:

> *Messala:* ... by proscription and bills of outlawry
> Octavius, Antony, and Lepidus
> Have put to death an hundred senators.

Among the dead, he confirms, is the respected politician and philosopher Cicero. The news comes as a shock, but the urgent business of planning their military response must continue. Brutus proposes marching their troops to Philippi immediately to confront their enemies. Cassius disagrees. They should keep their distance, and let their opponents wear themselves down in searching for them:

> *Cassius:* ... 'Tis better that the enemy seek us;
> So shall he waste his means,[1] weary his soldiers,
> Doing himself offence, whilst we, lying still,
> Are full of rest, defence, and nimbleness.

[1] *supplies*

Brutus, by contrast, argues that he and Cassius do not have the support of the general population in this territory. The local people are resentful of the presence of their army, and have only provided resources reluctantly. There is every possibility that Octavius and Antony will be able to pick up willing recruits as they march from Philippi towards Sardis, where Brutus and Cassius are now encamped. He repeats that they must head for Philippi as soon as possible.

Cassius tries to interrupt, but Brutus presses on. They have obtained all the resources they possibly can from their friends and allies, he insists, and their armies are in peak condition and ready to fight. Just as a ship takes advantage of the rising tide to set off on its voyage, they must take advantage of their present situation. If they do not, they will regret it for ever:

> *Brutus:* The enemy increaseth every day;
> We, at the height, are ready to decline.
> There is a tide in the affairs of men,
> Which, taken at the flood,[1] leads on to fortune;
> Omitted,[2] all the voyage of their life
> Is bound in shallows and in miseries.
> On such a full sea are we now afloat,
> And we must take the current when it serves,
> Or lose our ventures.[3]
>
> [1] *high point*
> [2] *if the opportunity is missed*
> [3] *lose everything, like a trader whose investments in merchandise have failed*

Cassius accepts without further argument: their armies will set out for Philippi tomorrow. By now it is very late. The two men decide to retire for a few hours' sleep, and they affectionately bid each other goodnight. Before he leaves the tent, Cassius expresses the heartfelt wish that they will never again fall out as they did earlier in the evening:

> *Cassius:* O my dear brother,
> This was an ill beginning of the night.
> Never come such division 'tween our souls!
> Let it not, Brutus.

Caesar returns

Brutus and young Lucius, his servant, remain in the tent. Brutus can see that his servant is sleepy, and asks him to call two others in; he may need someone to take a message to Cassius during the night.

Brutus decides to read before settling down to sleep. He also wants to hear some music, and asks Lucius to play his lute, apologizing for keeping him awake:

> *Brutus:* Canst thou hold up thy heavy eyes awhile,
> And touch thy instrument a strain[1] or two?
> *Lucius:* Ay, my lord, an't[2] please you.
> *Brutus:* It does, my boy.
> I trouble thee too much, but thou art willing.
> *Lucius:* It is my duty, sir.
> *Brutus:* I should not urge thy duty past thy might[3] ...
>
> [1] *play a tune*
> [2] *if it*
> [3] *I should not force you to do more than you are physically able to*

Lucius plays but, still holding his lute, is soon overtaken by sleep. Brutus carefully removes the instrument from the young man's arms, and returns to his book.

As Brutus reads, he notices that the candlelight is becoming dim. Looking round, he is horrified to see a strange apparition in the half-light: it is the ghost of Julius Caesar. As it approaches, he questions it, filled with dread. The ghost's answers are enigmatic and unnerving:

> *Brutus:* Art thou some god, some angel, or some devil,
> That mak'st my blood cold, and my hair to stare?[1]
> Speak to me what thou art.
> *Ghost:* Thy evil spirit, Brutus.
> *Brutus:* Why com'st thou?
> *Ghost:* To tell thee thou shalt see me at Philippi.
>
> [1] *stand on end*

The ghost vanishes. Agitated by the apparition, and anxious to know if the others in the tent witnessed it, he wakes Lucius and his companions; but they have all been sound asleep, and have seen nothing.

Now that the men are awake, however, he has an order for them. They are to pass a message on to Cassius: the advance on Philippi is to start as soon as possible.

The diary entry of a traveller from Switzerland who saw *Julius Caesar* in 1599, its first year of production, reveals some intriguing details:

"After lunch on September 21st, at about two o'clock, I went with my companions over the water, and in the house with the thatched roof witnessed an excellent performance of the tragedy of the first Emperor Julius Caesar with a cast of some fifteen people; when the play was over, they danced very marvellously and gracefully together, as is their custom, two dressed as men and two as women ... whoever cares to stand below only pays one English penny, while if he wants to sit he enters by another door, and pays another penny. If he desires to sit on a cushioned seat, where he not only sees everything well, but can also be seen, he pays yet another English penny at another door. During the performance food and drink are carried round the audience, so one can refresh oneself at one's own cost. The actors are most expensively and elaborately costumed ..."

Thomas Platter, *Travels in England*, 1599

A hostile meeting V, i

The armies of Octavius and Antony are encamped on the plains of Philippi. Antony had predicted that Brutus and Cassius would remain in the surrounding mountains rather than confronting their enemy directly, but he seems to have been proved wrong.

Octavius, confident that he and Antony can defeat their opponents in open warfare, is pleased:

> *Octavius:* Now, Antony, our hopes are answered.
> You said the enemy would not come down,
> But keep the hills and upper regions.
> It proves not so; their battles[1] are at hand;
> They mean to warn[2] us at Philippi here,
> Answering before we do demand of them.[3]
>
> [1] *battalions, armies*
> [2] *confront*
> [3] *responding before we have even challenged them to fight*

Antony still believes that their opponents are unwilling to face them. In coming down from the mountains, they are merely putting on a display of courage. However, a messenger now reports that a red banner has been hoisted in the enemy's ranks, meaning that all soldiers are to prepare for battle.

In response, Antony tells Octavius to lead his army slowly along the left side of the field of battle. Without explanation, however, Octavius contradicts him, and starts marching his forces to the right, ignoring Antony's angry reaction.

Meanwhile, Brutus and Cassius are coming out into the open, ahead of their troops. After a brief hesitation, Antony and Octavius do the same, and the four men meet on the plain, in the no-man's-land between the great armies. The parley quickly descends into acrimonious quarrelling. Antony reminds Brutus that he was speaking amicably to Caesar just before he stabbed him:

> *Brutus:* Words before blows: is it so, countrymen?
> *Octavius:* Not that we love words better, as you do.
> *Brutus:* Good words are better than bad strokes,[1] Octavius.
> *Antony:* In your bad strokes, Brutus, you give good words;
> Witness the hole you made in Caesar's heart,
> Crying, 'Long live! Hail, Caesar!'
>
> [1] *irrational violence*

As Antony becomes more and more angry and abusive, Cassius reminds Brutus, sarcastically, of his earlier advice to eliminate Antony along with Caesar:

> *Cassius:* Now, Brutus, thank yourself.
> This tongue had not offended so[1] to-day,
> If Cassius might have rul'd.
>
> [1] *Antony would not have been able to insult us in this way*

For his part, Octavius makes it clear that Caesar's killers can never be forgiven. In a dramatic gesture of determination, he draws his sword. As Caesar's chosen heir, he will either avenge his death or die in the attempt:

> *Octavius:* Look,
> I draw a sword against conspirators.
> When think you that the sword goes up[1] again?
> Never, till Caesar's three and thirty wounds
> Be well aveng'd; or till another Caesar
> Have added slaughter to the sword of traitors.[2]
>
> [1] *will be sheathed*
> [2] *until Octavius, Caesar's successor, has also been murdered by the conspirators*

Brutus retorts that he and the other conspirators are not traitors; in fact, dying at their hands would be the most honourable death that Octavius could wish for. Cassius then taunts his opponents, telling Octavius that he does not deserve such a noble death:

> *Cassius:* A peevish school-boy, worthless of such honour,
> Join'd with a masker and a reveller.[1]
>
> [1] *a debauched partygoer*

Shouting their defiance, Octavius and Antony return to join their armies. There will be no more delays: war is now inevitable.

Cassius has doubts

While Brutus talks to his second in command, Cassius calls for Messala. He mentions that it is his birthday. He then asks Messala to witness the fact that he has come to Philippi against his will; as he told Brutus, his preference was to force Antony and Octavius to seek them out in the mountains, rather than stake everything on one battle in the open field.

Cassius then confides in Messala that his attitude to omens has changed. In the past he never believed in such things, regarding them as foolish superstitions, but now he is unsure. He explains that while they were marching away from Sardis, two eagles had perched on the banner at the head of their legions. The eagles accompanied them on their march, feeding from the soldiers' hands; but this morning, at Philippi, they flew away. Instead, flocks of dark, menacing birds are circling overhead:

> *Cassius:* ... ravens, crows, and kites
> Fly o'er our heads, and downward look on us,
> As we were sickly prey;[1] their shadows seem
> A canopy most fatal,[2] under which
> Our army lies, ready to give up the ghost.
>
> [1] *as if we were weak creatures about to die and become their prey*
> [2] *ominous, indicating that disaster is imminent*

However, Cassius is not entirely convinced that such events have any meaning. He is in good spirits, he assures Messala, and ready to face whatever dangers may come their way.

Brutus now returns. Cassius expresses the hope that they will both live, as friends, to a ripe old age. However, life is unpredictable; and if the worst should happen in the forthcoming battle, they will not meet again.

Cassius then asks Brutus a direct question: what has he resolved to do if they are defeated? Brutus's answer, by contrast, is lengthy and unclear. As a Stoic, he explains, he is against suicide; whatever happens, he will patiently let fate take its course. At the same time, it would be unthinkable to allow himself to be dragged captive by the triumphant Octavius and Antony through the streets of Rome. In any event, today's conflict will be decisive:

> *Brutus:* ... this same day
> Must end that work the ides of March begun;
> And whether we shall meet again I know not.
> Therefore our everlasting farewell take.
> For ever, and for ever, farewell, Cassius.
> If we do meet again, why, we shall smile;
> If not, why then this parting was well made.

The two leaders leave to prepare for battle.

A crucial command   V, ii

The opposing armies have come out into the plains of Philippi, and battle is under way. From his vantage point, Brutus can see that, on the far side of the battlefield, facing Cassius, Octavius' troops are weakening and vulnerable.

Brutus calls for Messala and orders him to ride at full speed to Cassius. His instruction to Cassius is clear: now is the time for a combined all-out attack on Octavius.

Cassius gives up hope   V, iii

The sudden attack on Octavius has not had the desired effect. Following a successful assault, Brutus's troops have become undisciplined, and have started looting instead of fighting. Antony's legions have taken advantage of the confusion, and are surrounding Cassius' army.

Many of Cassius' soldiers have deserted. Even his standard-bearer tried to retreat; Cassius has executed him and seized the standard himself. Titinius, Cassius' right-hand man, blames Brutus for the disarray:

> *Cassius:* This ensign here of mine was turning back;
> I slew the coward, and did take it from him.
> *Titinius:* O Cassius, Brutus gave the word too early,
> Who, having some advantage on Octavius,
> Took it too eagerly; his soldiers fell to spoil,[1]
> Whilst we by Antony are all enclos'd.

> [1] *destruction, plunder*

Pindarus, Cassius' servant, now rushes towards them, shouting frantically. Cassius' own encampment has been overrun by Antony's soldiers. Cassius chooses to stay where he is:

> *Pindarus:* Fly further off, my lord, fly further off!
> Mark Antony is in your tents, my lord.
> Fly, therefore, noble Cassius, fly far off!
> *Cassius:* This hill is far enough. Look, look, Titinius!
> Are those my tents where I perceive the fire?
> *Titinius:* They are, my lord.

Cassius spots some troops in the distance, and sends Titinius to confirm whether they are friendly or hostile. He asks Pindarus to go further up the hill to observe Titinius' reaction; his own eyesight is poor. As Pindarus leaves, it becomes clear that Cassius is pessimistic about the outcome of today's battle.

It is ironic, reflects Cassius, that he should die today, on his birthday:

Cassius: This day I breathed first. Time is come round,
And where I did begin, there shall I end.
My life is run his compass.[1]

[1] *its full circuit*

Cassius' fears are confirmed as Pindarus, shouting from the distance, describes how Titinius, charging towards the troops, is surrounded and captured. The soldiers' victorious cheers can be clearly heard.

Cassius calls Pindarus back. Overcome with shame at allowing Titinius to be captured, and convinced that defeat is imminent, Cassius asks his servant to perform one final duty. He reminds Pindarus how he had been captured in battle in the distant eastern land of Parthia; now, he promises, his enslavement is over. He hands him his sword:

Cassius: Now be a freeman; and with this good sword,
That ran through Caesar's bowels, search this bosom.
... Guide thou the sword. – Caesar, thou art reveng'd,
Even with the sword that kill'd thee. [*Dies.*]

"Julius Caesar appears in only three scenes of the play. In the first scene of the third act he dies. Where he does appear, the poet seems anxious to insist upon the weakness rather than the strength of Caesar ... This bodily presence of Caesar is but of secondary importance, and may be supplied when it actually passes away, by Octavius as its substitute. It is the spirit of Caesar which is the dominant power of the tragedy ... he who has been weak now rises as pure spirit, strong and terrible, and avenges himself upon the conspirators."

Edward Dowden, *Shakspere: A Critical Study of His Mind and Art*, 1875

Pindarus wishes that he could have achieved his liberty in some other way; however, he has obeyed his master, and is now free. He runs from the battlefield, vowing never again to become involved in the affairs of Rome.

Another casualty

It now becomes clear that Pindarus was mistaken. Titinius has not been captured by the enemy, and is now coming back, with Messala, to join Cassius.

The day is drawing to a close. Messala tells Titinius that although Cassius' army has been overcome by Antony, Brutus has triumphed against the troops commanded by Octavius. This news should give some comfort to Cassius, they hope: but at this moment they discover Cassius' lifeless body on the ground. Titinius realizes what has happened, and blames himself for his leader's death:

> *Messala:* Is not that he?
> *Titinius:* No, this was he, Messala,
> But Cassius is no more. O setting sun,
> As in thy red rays thou dost sink to night,
> So in his red blood Cassius' day is set.
> ... Mistrust of my success[1] hath done this deed.
>
> [1] *doubt about the outcome of my mission*

Messala assures his friend that it was not his fault; it was despair about the outcome of the day's fighting in general that drove Cassius to suicide, he believes, not Titinius' task in particular.

When Messala has left to break the bad news to Brutus, Titinius addresses his dead friend. The troops that he encountered earlier were friends, not enemies, and their shouts were of welcome, not anger. Fresh from their triumph over Octavius' army, they had with them a victory wreath which, at Brutus's request, was to be given to Cassius.

Titinius' last act is to put the wreath on his leader's brow. He ends his life with the same sword that killed both Caesar and Cassius:

Titinius: Why didst thou send me forth, brave Cassius?
Did I not meet thy friends, and did not they
Put on my brows this wreath of victory,
And bid me give it to thee? Didst thou not hear their shouts?
Alas, thou hast misconstrued every thing.
But hold thee, take this garland on thy brow;
Thy Brutus bid me give it thee, and I
Will do his bidding.
 … This is a Roman's part: [1]
Come, Cassius' sword, and find Titinius' heart. [*Dies.*]

[1] *act that is fitting for a noble Roman*

Messala now returns, bringing Brutus to pay his respects to his dead companion. He is dismayed to find that Titinius too has taken his own life:

Brutus: O Julius Caesar, thou art mighty yet! [1]
Thy spirit walks abroad,[2] and turns our swords
In our own proper entrails.

[1] *still*
[2] *everywhere, unconfined*

Brutus fears that an era of Roman greatness is coming to an end. He is devastated by the loss of his lifelong friend, but there is no time for mourning now:

Brutus: Are yet two Romans living such as these?
The last of all the Romans, fare thee well!
It is impossible that ever Rome
Should breed thy fellow. Friends, I owe moe [1] tears
To this dead man than you shall see me pay.
I shall find time, Cassius, I shall find time.

[1] *more*

He orders his followers to take the body away to a nearby island. The funeral will not take place here at Philippi; the battle is not yet over, and morale must be maintained.

An important prisoner
V, iv

Having defeated Octavius' army, Brutus is now leading the fight against Antony. This time, however, Brutus's opponent has the upper hand, and Brutus is hurrying around the battlefield, rallying his troops.

In the thick of the battle, Lucilius, one of Brutus's officers, cries out that he is Brutus, in an attempt to confuse the enemy and protect his leader. Antony's soldiers, about to slaughter him, instead seize him as a valuable hostage. Soon Antony himself arrives on the scene. He recognizes Lucilius, and orders his men to treat their captive respectfully:

> *Antony:* This is not Brutus, friend; but, I assure you,
> A prize no less in worth. Keep this man safe;
> Give him all kindness. I had rather have
> Such men as my friends than enemies.

Antony sends his soldiers off in search of Brutus.

Final farewells
V, v

The battle is going Antony's way, and Brutus knows that defeat is inevitable. It is dark by now, and he has withdrawn to a secluded area of the plain with a few loyal followers.

Brutus is ready to die. He quietly asks each of his followers to kill him, but they refuse. He reveals to one of them, Volumnius, that he has had a premonition of his fate. The night before the battle, Caesar's ghost appeared to him for a second time:

> *Brutus:* The ghost of Caesar hath appear'd to me
> Two several[1] times by night: at Sardis once,
> And this last night, here in Philippi fields.
> I know my hour is come.
> *Volumnius:*   Not so, my lord.

Brutus: Nay, I am sure it is, Volumnius.
Thou seest the world, Volumnius, how it goes:
Our enemies have beat us to the pit.[2]
It is more worthy to leap in ourselves
Than tarry till they push us.

[1] *separate*
[2] *trap into which wild animals are driven*

Volumnius too refuses to kill Brutus. The noise of battle is getting louder, and Antony's troops are not far off. Brutus says a last farewell to his followers. He has always been blessed with loyal friends and supporters, he reflects. And even in defeat, he feels that his life is worthier than the lives of those who will bring about the end of the Republic:

Brutus: Countrymen,
My heart doth joy that yet in all my life
I found no man but he was true[1] to me.
I shall have glory by this losing day
More than Octavius and Mark Antony
By this vile conquest shall attain unto.

[1] *who was not true*

The enemy is now very close, and Brutus urges his followers to retreat. They finally do so, except for one man, Strato, who had been asleep while Brutus was addressing the others. Brutus asks him to carry out the task that the others had refused. Strato consents, and holds out his leader's sword as Brutus throws himself onto it.

As Brutus dies, he calls on Caesar to be at rest in his grave. Brutus is far more willing to kill himself, he proclaims, than he ever was to kill Caesar:

Brutus: Caesar, now be still;
I kill'd not thee with half so good a will.

> "... both Brutus and Cassius seem to find release from some not fully understood oppression of their spirits only when they die upon the swords with which they killed Caesar, and with his name on their lips."
>
> T. S. Dorsch, Introduction to the Arden edition of *Julius Caesar*, 1955

A new regime

Antony and Octavius now arrive on the scene with their troops. With them are Messala and Lucilius, who have both been captured.

Messala recognizes Strato, Brutus's follower. Strato announces, defiantly, that his master has chosen death rather than captivity. On seeing Brutus's body, Lucilius remarks that it is fitting that his leader has died in this way:

> *Messala:*   Strato, where is thy master?
> *Strato:*   Free from the bondage you are in, Messala.
>   The conquerors can but make a fire of him;
>   For Brutus only[1] overcame himself,
>   And no man else hath honour by his death.
> *Lucilius:* So Brutus should be found.
>
> [1] *Brutus alone*

Octavius declares that he will accept all Brutus's followers as his own, and Strato agrees to his offer.

Antony pays a final tribute to his opponent:

Antony: This was the noblest Roman of them all.
All the conspirators save only he
Did that[1] they did in envy[2] of great Caesar;
He only, in a general honest thought
And common good to all, made one of them.[3]

[1] *what*
[2] *malice, animosity*
[3] *he joined them out of honourable concern for the greater good of the people*

Brutus's body will be treated with the utmost respect and given an honourable burial, confirms Octavius.

Now that the final remains of Brutus's army have been overcome, the conflict has come to an end. Octavius looks to the future:

Octavius: Within my tent his bones to-night shall lie,
Most like a soldier, order'd honourably.
So call the field to rest,[1] and let's away,
To part the glories[2] of this happy[3] day.

[1] *announce the end of hostilities*
[2] *divide the rewards*
[3] *fortunate*

Caesar's murder has been avenged: the civil war is over, and the victors will share the spoils.

Acknowledgements

The following publications have proved invaluable as sources of factual information and critical insight:

- John F. Andrews, Introduction to the Everyman edition of *Julius Caesar*, J. M. Dent, 1993

- Jonathan Bate, *Soul of the Age*, Penguin Books, 2008

- Mary Beard, *SPQR: A History of Ancient Rome*, Profile Books, 2015

- Charles Boyce, *Shakespeare A to Z*, Roundtable Press, 1990

- T. S. Dorsch, Introduction to the Arden edition of *Julius Caesar*, Methuen, 1955

- Alison Findlay, *Women in Shakespeare*, Bloomsbury Arden Shakespeare, 2014

- Harley Granville-Barker, *Prefaces to Shakespeare Volume II*, B. T. Batsford, 1930

- John Gross, *After Shakespeare*, Oxford University Press, 2002

- Maynard Mack, *Everybody's Shakespeare*, Bison Books, 1993

- Laurie Maguire and Emma Smith, *30 Great Myths about Shakespeare*, Wiley-Blackwell, 2013

- Norman Sanders, Introduction to the New Penguin edition of *Julius Caesar*, Penguin Books, 1967

- James Shapiro, *1599: A Year in the Life of William Shakespeare*, Faber and Faber, 2005

- Michael Wood, *In Search of Shakespeare*, BBC Books, 2003

All quotations from *Julius Caesar* are taken from the Arden Shakespeare.

Guides currently available in the *Shakespeare Handbooks* series are:

- **Antony & Cleopatra** (ISBN 978 1 899747 02 3, £4.95)
- **As You Like It** (ISBN 978 1 899747 00 9, £4.95)
- **Hamlet** (ISBN 978 1 899747 07 8, £4.95)
- **Henry IV, Part 1** (ISBN 978 1 899747 05 4, £4.95)
- **Julius Caesar** (ISBN 978 1 899747 11 5, £4.95)
- **King Lear** (ISBN 978 1 899747 03 0, £4.95)
- **Macbeth** (ISBN 978 1 899747 04 7, £4.95)
- **A Midsummer Night's Dream** (ISBN 978 1 899747 09 2, £4.95)
- **Romeo & Juliet** (ISBN 978 1 899747 10 8, £4.95)
- **The Tempest** (ISBN 978 1 899747 08 5, £4.95)
- **Twelfth Night** (ISBN 978 1 899747 01 6, £4.95)

www.shakespeare-handbooks.com

Prices correct at time of going to press. Whilst every effort is made to keep prices low, Upstart Crow Publications reserves the right to show new retail prices on covers which may differ from those previously advertised in the text or elsewhere.